AIKIDO *sketch* DIARY

AIKIDO *sketch* DIARY

Dojo 365 Days

Gaku Homma

Translated by

Yutaka Kikuchi

Frog, Ltd.
Berkeley, California

Aikido Sketch Diary: Dojo 365 Days

Copyright © 1994 by Gaku Homma. No portion of this book, except for brief review, may be reproduced in any form without written permission of the publisher. For information contact Frog, Ltd. c/o North Atlantic Books.

Published by Frog, Ltd.
and Domo Productions/Nippon Kan
    988 Cherokee Street
    Denver, Colorado 80204

Frog, Ltd. books are distributed by
North Atlantic Books
P.O. Box 12327
Berkeley, California 94712

Cover art and illustrations by Gaku Homma
Cover and book design by Paula Morrison
Typeset by Catherine Campaigne

Printed in the United States of America by Malloy Lithographing

Library of Congress Cataloging-in-Publication Data
Homma, Gaku, 1950–
        Aikido sketch diary : dojo 365 days / Gaku Homma
            p.   cm.
        ISBN 1-883319-22-6
        1. Aikido—Training—United States.   2. Dōjō school—Case studies.
    3. Japan—Popular culture—Zen influences.   I. Title.
    GV1114.35.H65   1994
    796.8'154—dc20
                                                                94-19558
                                                                CIP

1   2   3   4   5   6   7   8   9 / 98   97   96   95   94

Acknowledgments

I WOULD LIKE to extend my sincere appreciation to all the volunteer staff and students of Nippon Kan.

Your activities in training are not limited to Nippon Kan but are extended into your communities. You are truly twentieth-century martial artists. I decided to write this book in order to introduce your wonderful activities to the public. Witnessing Aikido, an aspect of Japanese culture, being practiced here by Americans like yourselves, and seeing the spirit of Aikido being restored in society, cannot help but deepen my respect for this country and the American people.

I profoundly appreciate the fact that I, a Japanese Aikidoist, have the opportunity to live in the United States and practice Aikido among you.

Gaku Homma

Table of Contents

Section II. Practice

Section III. Annual Events

Section IV. Dojo Operations

Section V. Other Aspects of the Dojo

Editor's Notes

THIS BOOK IS a collection of drawings and text by Gaku Homma, the founder of Aikido Nippon Kan. Homma Sensei is a man of many talents, but the English language may be his greatest challenge. Students joke that it takes about the same amount of time to finally understand Homma Sensei's English as it does to earn a black belt! This, however, does not seem to worry him much, and he is ingenious in finding ways to communicate and express himself. One very important way he overcomes the hurdles of verbal communication is through action. As a student of nine years, I have watched Homma Sensei repeatedly lead his students into action, both practicing Aikido on the mat and engaging in a multitude of projects off the mat. He is often asked why he instigates so many projects. Homma Sensei usually jokes that everyone else has a regular job with Aikido as their hobby, but since his job *is* Aikido, he is constantly looking for new challenges because he needs a hobby too!

This book is a diary of Nippon Kan's activities and events. Whether digging in the vegetable garden, writing a cookbook, building a new Japanese room, publishing Aikido books, or cooking and washing dishes at the Homeless Shelter, Homma Sensei is forever doing something, fixing something, or planning something else.

Sketches are a natural tool by which Homma Sensei can express a multitude of thoughts and ideas. One very good example is the cover of this book, a drawing entitled "After 10th *Dan*." This was done in response to questions from students who seemed overly concerned about rank and promotions. Homma Sensei uses a lot of humor in his drawings, from the subtle to the exaggerated. Even the most serious and philosophical of his sketches contain a hint of humor and a sense of heart. This flexibility in perspective is well-suited to the Aikidoist.

Homma Sensei very much enjoyed working on this book and delighted in showing preliminary sketches to the office staff. Since we ourselves were the subject of many of the sketch parodies, this resulted in many a laugh—even if at our own expense! While he is not a professional artist, Homma Sensei has had some experience with drawing. He produced all of the sketches for his book *The Folk Art of Japanese Country Cooking: A Traditional Diet for Today's World,* and he also furnished the preliminary sketches for *Children and the Martial Arts: An Aikido Point of View* and *Aikido for Life.* He claims drawing is not his best subject, but his unlabored style lends even more charm to the sketches themselves.

Nippon Kan's name appears frequently in this book and there is a reason for that. Homma Sensei has expressed many times that there are many different kinds of *dojos* and organizations, each with its own philosophy and approach to learning. Out of respect for others, Homma Sensei emphasizes that this book does not represent the entire Aikido community, but offers a glimpse into *dojo* life at Nippon Kan.

These days, with computer networks, newsletters, and the like, there is an overflow of information on Aikido. *Dojos* spring up like dandelions, and so many new *Senseis* are emerging that if you closed your eyes and tossed a pebble, you would likely hit one. There is a need to reflect a little on what is truly important about our practice and about the experience of training in a *dojo.* In its entirety, this book offers a good look at the workings of Nippon Kan. In its pages are valuable insights into what the word "*dojo*" might really mean and have to offer us. These glimpses serve as small candles, shedding light on important points we otherwise might have missed.

Most martial arts books are presented in a very serious tone. This book shows us that such severity is not the only way to approach the study of the martial arts. As a reminder of this, Ponk, the *dojo* dog appears frequently throughout this book. Ponk was born April 7, 1989 and is listed in the *dojo* computers as holding the rank of 3rd *kyu*.

Enjoy your reading.

Emily Busch
Editor

Foreword

As THOSE WHO practice Aikido, where do we look to practice? Where do we look for the path of practice known as *shugyo?* During the 1960s and 70s many Americans, especially young people, began to question a world defined by science, materialism, and the Western values with which they had been raised. Many began searching for alternatives, looking for meaning in the Eastern ideas and philosophy that were being introduced to America. Exposure to Eastern thinking was widely introduced to America by the military after World War II. By the time the war in Vietnam was at its height, the younger generations at home had joined forces with their friends overseas, culminating in a peak influx of Eastern thinking.

The art of Aikido also rode this incoming wave as it was introduced to the United States. Now, forty years later, where has the practice of Aikido found its place in the United States of the 90s?

In order to recognize the place of Aikido in the United States today, we must first understand how we are approaching our study of this art. From my Japanese point of view, I can see that there are definite distinctions between Western and Eastern approaches to the pursuit of understanding a subject. A Western approach is often very clinical and analytical, and uses a kind of mental laboratory to dissect, analyze, and draw theories and conclusions on information presented. I have witnessed those who have tried to understand the teachings of Morehei Ueshiba, the founder of Aikido, by trying to reconstruct him "Terminator-style" from fragments of scattered information gathered from a multitude of conflicting sources.

This has not only happened with Aikido. As they have made their way to the United States, many Eastern practices have undergone greater or lesser degrees of transformation. This sometimes depended on how much marketing-for-profit was a factor in their introduction.

I want to emphasize that the information available in the United States about Aikido is somewhat different than the Aikido originally created by Morehei Ueshiba in Japan. This is an important point to keep in mind while studying the available materials on the subject.

That ideas and customs adapt and change as they are introduced to a new environment is a natural process of cultural evolution. This phenomenon is not limited to the United States. Cultural adaptation has played a major role in Japan's historical past, as well.

For example, Buddhism, which was to profoundly influence not only Japanese beliefs but its culture and customs, originally came from China. So did the arts of tea ceremony and flower arrangement. Today, these are all an integral part of Japanese culture, but the process has taken more than 1,300 years.

During a recent Aikido seminar, I related a discovery I had just made to the students. I had just learned that the image of Santa Claus—the cute, kindly gentleman with the red suit and white beard—had actually been created by an artist for a soft drink company. This advertising campaign, meant to inspire holiday spirit (and spending), had been launched less than sixty years ago. Everyone looked at me in surprise; they had all been unaware of this fact. Everyone recognizes the image of Santa Claus but takes for granted the origin of that image. The look on the student's faces was like that of a child in a Norman Rockwell painting who had just found Santa's outfit in his daddy's bottom dresser drawer! The red-suited Santa is very popular today; in fact, he can be seen in churches, schools, department stores, and hospitals all over the world. Nice uncles dress up as Santa and give out presents to children at community centers. Even other soft drink companies have a red-suited Santa in their ad campaigns now. This is a good example of how culture can be widely changed in just a few year's time.

Aikido has been taught in the United States for about forty years. It isn't necessary to go back to its beginnings even in this country to see how fast it has grown and changed. In the last ten years, there has been so much change that at this rate we may soon be wearing uniforms and *hakamas* (a pant-like over-garment) red in color like Santa's clothes.

Let's go back to how the pursuit of understanding may differ from a Western and Eastern point of view. Generally speaking, a basic principle of Western thought lies in the assumption that in order to understand something, we must seek out and define its origin and development logically when at all possible. Astronomy, mathematics, cultural and historical anthropology, and other analytical sciences have been developed along these premises. Christianity has also been deeply ingrained in the evolution of Western thought and culture.

Conversely, for the Eastern mind understanding comes through doing and experiencing. Only by emptying the mind of discursive thought (in Japanese this process is called *Mu*) can one reach understanding. Buddhism and Shintoism are important influences in this concept. *Do* ("the path" or "way"), is the way of unlimited action. A Zen parable illustrates this idea. One day, a cow ran away from a temple. Since the cow is a sacred religious symbol, all the people from the village came to the temple to organize a search for the lost cow. The *Roshi* (master priest of the Zen temple) listened patiently to the villagers as they formed their plans for the search. He waited for the appropriate moment to speak but it never came, and finally the villagers left to search the surrounding mountains.

Long after the sun had set, the tired villagers straggled back toward the temple without the cow. Everyone gathered around the *Roshi* and hung their heads. "Where is the cow?" asked the *Roshi*. "The canyons were long and deep," said a villager, "and divided into side canyon after side canyon. Soon we didn't have enough people to search every path the cow might have taken. We lost him." "The cow is here," replied the *Roshi,* smiling. "You are riding the cow now. See? You are riding the cow."

If we alter the metaphor and make the cow a symbol of our human spirit or mind, this story gives us an interesting perspective to ponder.

If Aikido develops in America strictly from a Western viewpoint, it may be truly difficult to understand. Many different analytical approaches have been used to try and understand founder Morihei Ueshiba and his teachings, even going so far as attempting to analyze a piece of cloth from his garments.

Today there is more and more written on Aikido in the United States. I have seen articles on everything from "Flying Rainbow *Ki* Power" to "Rambo-style" secret death techniques. The latest computer network technology now allows anyone, regardless of the level of their experience, to transmit their theories on Aikido around the globe in seconds.

Some may be inspired by these articles and transmissions, but I fear they may also result in illusion and confusion. Perhaps some of my concerns are linked to the fact that I am a Japanese instructor coming from an Eastern background.

Japanese instructors and American students can and have interpreted concepts and ideas differently. For example, if you ask an American student where his mind is, he would usually point to his head. If asked the same question in Japan, a person would point to her heart!

Mr. Yutaka Kikuchi, the translator of this and other books I have written, brought an interesting point to my attention. Aikido books originally written in Japanese and translated to English by Westerners are often interpreted with influences from Christianity and even imagery from modern movies and literature. Although there is absolutely nothing wrong with Christianity, or movies for that matter, their influence results in a slightly different perspective than what was originally intended.

For example, Founder Morehei Ueshiba left many *doka* (didactic poems) which include concepts such as God, Universe, and Nature. Such concepts are open to vast interpretations. It is natural for students in the United States to try to understand the meaning of these poems to further their understanding of their practice of Aikido. The Founder's poems have been translated, disassembled, analyzed, discussed, and theorized upon. Pieces of poems have been examined individually and theories developed until primary elements of Aikido philosophy have emerged independent of one another. Some of these new philosophies seem to have left the realm of earthly reality and are no longer firmly planted on the ground.

In Japan, these poems are studied differently. The *doka* are viewed whole, without much analysis. They become a frame of mind that is experienced. How is this done? By just doing it. For us as Aikidoka, this can be applied to our practice. By just doing—continuing our practice—we can achieve this experiential frame of mind.

The concept of God in the views of Shintoism as Morihei Ueshiba understood it is completely different in origin and existence than the concept of God in Western Christian thought. This is very important to understand if we want to interpret the Founder's philosophies with as little distortion as possible.

Even in Japan the concept of God has had an interesting history. From the end of the Edo period (1603–1867) through the Meiji period (1868–1900), the new Meiji government attempted desperately to change Japanese culture and adopt the highly regarded and fashionable ways of Europe especially, and the United States. In those times, the *Samurai* put down their swords and wore their hair in the latest Western fashion. Kimonos were accessorized with silk top hats, canes, and Western shoes. So obsessed was Japan with Western ways that in 1873 the Secretary of Education took bold steps towards Westernizing intrinsic elements of Japan's education system. Even the definition of the Japanese word *Kami* ("God") was changed to the definition found in a leading English dictionary of the time—a definition of God as originally put forth in the Old Testament of the Bible.

The Meiji Era was a rather dubious time for Japan, and although these major changes in religious definitions were not well received, traces of them still remain today. This makes it all the more confusing for the Western translator to arrive at true meanings when the Japanese text has already been altered in this way from its original form.

This book is not about religion, so my discussion will be limited here. The point I wish to make is that we need to approach our study of Aikido with a very open mind—open even to examining the way in which we approach the study itself.

As we learn and practice Aikido together, learning the physical movements is only part of our practice. To not realize that the perception and understanding of Aikido may differ among those practicing can cause misunderstandings. An action that looks the same may not be the same at all to different people, at different times, in different places— or even to different people at the same time, in the very same place.

For example, there is a proverb common in both the United States and Japan: "A rolling stone gathers no moss." If a Japanese instructor were to say this, he would probably receive nods of acknowledgment and understanding from the American students. And yet these same students two months later may leave to pursue other interests, exactly the situation that the instructor was counseling against by using this expression. The Western perception that it is normal for students to move around a lot and change their interests quickly is perplexing to the Japanese way of thinking. In Japan, it is considered much more valuable for the stone *not* to move, to stay in one place until a beautiful mantle of moss can grow on it. This is the meaning of the Japanese proverb. Yet here in the United States, the same words take on an entirely different meaning—a rolling stone stays fresh and clean by not staying long in one place.

If problems do arise between those practicing Aikido together, the cause can usually be traced to a fundamental difference in understanding and interpreting what Aikido is or should be. If those involved in a disagreement feel very attached to their practice of Aikido and how they perceive that it should be practiced, this can lead to tension between people that is not easily mended.

Here are two good examples of the difference between a Western and Eastern approach toward Aikido practice. An American student who has practiced for many years with a Japanese instructor suddenly quits his practice. Or, an American student dreams of going to Japan to practice as an *uchideshi* (live-in-student) at a traditional Japanese *dojo*, only to find they can't fit in because it is nothing like they thought it would be. Both cases are the results of failing to understand that there are profound differences in cultural perspective and methods. In a most unfortunate scenario, a disillusioned student may leave a *dojo* and go his own way, filled with bitterness. "I love practicing Aikido, but I can't understand *Sensei's* mind. I think Aikido should be like _____."

At my *dojo,* Nippon Kan, our logo is an image of a child riding a cow. This image comes from the *Ju Gyu Zu* ("The Chart of Ten Cows") created by Zen master Kakuan Shion *Roshi* in twelfth-century China. Our logo, called *Ki Gyu Kika* ("The Cow Returns Home"), is taken from the sixth image in the series.

The cow is a symbol for human consciousness or mind. This chart is a symbolic explanation of life. Remember the Zen story about the cow that was missing from the temple? At the end of the story, the *Roshi* told the villagers "You are riding the cow now. See? You are riding the cow." This realization is a basic part of Nippon Kan's philosophy. It is an idea I have stressed in my other works on Aikido, including *Aikido for Life* and *Children and the Martial Arts: An Aikido Point of View.* Put simply, it is this: practice is here, now. There is so much we can learn just by practicing, sweating, and moving.

Nippon Kan is a small hometown *dojo.* Although it has about 250 practicing members, I still think of it as small. In the United States, there are large Aikido organizations made up of many *dojos.* In comparison, we are very small indeed. A good analogy for Nippon Kan might be that of a small-town non-franchised hamburger stand.

In Japan there is an old proverb: "The frog who lives his life inside a well will never know the ocean." Let's examine the meaning of this. A tiny frog born in a deep well knows only the world that he can see and feel around him. To him, the heavens consist of the circle of sky he can see above, and the ocean is the water in the well.

To understand this proverb, we need to think of ourselves as this frog. On one hand, this proverb can be taken as a warning against making judgments based on limited experience—the frog may seem a fool for living in the well. Or, the frog might take the challenge to climb his way to the top of the well to try to grasp the vastness of the skies above him and the oceans below. This effort may be thought commendable, but there can be a high price to pay. Many have fallen prey to the stress, sacrifices, and doubts that result in spending one's time in pursuit of unattainable understanding. No one has yet been able to fully embrace the limitlessness of the heavens or drink in the entire ocean in this manner, for such a search is endless.

So, if we look at it from another point of view, the frog may be wiser than we think. He will never suffer the turmoil and strife of trying to survive in life's tumultuous larger oceans. Maybe the frog would say to us, "My well is just fine, thank you; I have no need to find the ocean since I am happy here just as I am."

Living life day by day down in his well, the frog imagines that the circle of sky he can see above him is the whole of the heavens, and that the water below him is the whole of the oceans. "This is enough," exclaims the frog, accepting his small space with gratitude and contentment. In doing so, the well of the little frog becomes unlimited in space without boundaries.

For human beings, "liveable space" is created by accepting and finding satisfaction in the world around us, which in turn can give us unlimited opportunity. If one enters this calm infinite space and quietly thinks about life, what once seemed a small space becomes filled with mountains, flowers, and the sound of birds—a whole world is created.

Bodhidharma, one of the founders of Zen Buddhism, found enlightenment by sitting on a rock for nine years. His discovery was that happiness and understanding can be found in the present, in the very place where one is standing. Enlightenment is not out there somewhere on the horizon. If we do not live in the present, there can be no tomorrow. In this manner, my life and Nippon Kan have been created. My practice of Aikido and my daily life are embraced in this spirit. Sometimes it may feel a little lonely staying in our "well" but that well's empty space offers infinite possibilities for ideas to be born and developed. This book is a one-year chronicle of one small independent *dojo* called Nippon Kan. As you read, please keep in mind the meaning of the story of the frog living in the well.

Aikido Sketch Diary: Dojo 365 Days goes into great detail about Nippon Kan's practices, projects, and organizational structure. This is not because I wished to write an advertisement for Nippon Kan. My intention is to offer ideas to all Aikidoka, especially those involved in trying to run a *dojo*. Many times, groups very dedicated to practicing Aikido run into small obstacles that turn into major problems. I have hoped to offer our experiences at Nippon Kan as possible solutions to problems or as ideas for growth and development. All of the stories in the following pages are true. They have all come from my experiences developing Nippon Kan over the last fifteen years.

As Aikidoka in a rapidly changing modern world, I think we need to continually ask ourselves, What is *shugyo?*—daring, I think, to jump into the well. Looking around at the Aikido community, I feel it may be time for this kind of reflection. In the hopes that this small-town hamburger stand can offer ideas that might help benefit the Aikido community, I present this book.

The words "Nippon Kan" appear frequently in this book simply because this is the name of my *dojo*. I would not presume to be able to speak for all of Aikido and feel it would be quite discourteous to other *dojos* to do so. I limit my views to what I have actually experienced at

Nippon Kan. Each *dojo* has different ideas, values, and unique opportunities. I do believe, however, that *dojos* around the world all have special dedicated volunteers that keep them running as smoothly as the one described in this book.

Today, Aikido is sometimes associated with special spiritual powers like "*ki* power" or other forms of magic. For many years I have tried to put a limit on notions of mystery, insinuations that Aikido has some link with powers of the universe or is in some way supernatural. I sometimes feel like I am going against popular trends in contemporary Aikido theory, but I prefer to stay with practical, traditional teaching methods. At Nippon Kan, one principle of our practice is "Each Day, Step by Step." Where you are standing—the ground under your feet—is your place of practice, your *dojo*. It is not out there somewhere in another dimension or universe.

For the past fifteen years, I have dedicated my practice to finding a way to blend a "Japanese Way of Thinking" with an "American Way of Thinking." I have made many discoveries on this journey, and some have become themes for study at Nippon Kan. "Motion and Sweat," "Look Where You are Standing," "Just as You are Naturally," "Beyond the Mat," "Beyond *Ki*," and "Be Kind to Yourself" have all been themes over the years.

Aikido Sketch Diary is a documentary of a full year of practice at Nippon Kan. Each of the five sections outlines an aspect of life at this traditionally-styled *dojo*. The calligraphy on the front cover of this book was done by master calligrapher Rev. Ryotoku Sato, a priest from the Zen temple of Naruse, our exchange village in Japan. The calligraphy under each sketch in this book was done by Hideki Sugawara, an exchange student from Naruse sent to study at Nippon Kan.

The first outlines the life of the *uchideshi* (live-in students) who have chosen to pursue an intensive course of Aikido training. Basically, life as an *uchideshi* is an exposure to the life of practice experienced by the pioneers of martial arts in Japan. It is by no means an easy lifestyle; it is a twenty-four-hour-a-day responsibility.

The *uchideshi* program is not for everyone. It is not meant to turn students into the kind of martial art heroes dreamed up in fantasy. A *dojo* is not a shelter but a place of learning for those who have already begun to develop the skills it takes to be successful in the world. An *uchideshi* student must be able to adapt and learn in an environment that is completely different than what is normally encountered in the United States. For those who can take care of themselves, there is much that can be learned in the *uchideshi* program. One word of advice: "Practice is not for gain."

The second section of this book is an anthology on "Practice," describing the different levels of Aikido instruction available at the Nippon Kan *dojo*. The many programs that have been developed over the years required a lot of detailed, deliberate, extensive planning and hard work.

If a plant is left in a window and not moved, the leaves and flowers will turn and face the outside, seeking light. Instructors must work very hard to make the *dojo* a creative and challenging place. They must create so much energy that even the plants outside grow in toward the windows to see what's going on! A message to senior students and to those involved in operating a *dojo:* what is most important is "Motion and Sweat."

The third section highlights annual events at Nippon Kan. An important part of the yearly events schedule is participation and involvement in serving the surrounding community. Practicing "Beyond the Mat" is an important way for students to learn more about themselves as they relate to others.

The fourth section focuses on how the *dojo* itself is operated, introducing guidelines used at Nippon Kan for more efficient management. To insure students a relaxed, safe, and comfortable place to practice, secure and efficient management systems are vital. Depicted in this section are hard-working volunteers busy at their posts. Working to keep the *dojo* running smoothly is also part of daily practice.

The final section covers other aspects of training, paying tribute to all the people behind the scenes who help make a *dojo* successful and happy. Their efforts cannot be forgotten.

You may be a little surprised to find a traditional subject like the study of martial arts portrayed with cartoons. Actually, to truly understand the martial arts, a sense of humor is an absolute requirement. Today's young people receive information from numerous sources that distracts them from reading books. I have tried to make this book easy to read and entertaining, as well as thought-provoking.

Read in its entirety, this book gives a general view of a year of practice at Nippon Kan. As I have mentioned, important to understanding this kind of experience is the realization that where we look for our path of practice is right under our own feet. It can't be found buried in the annals of Aikido history, nor lost in the pursuit of some celestial consciousness.

The Founder, Morehei Ueshiba, has said that for Aikido to grow it must be allowed to do so freely. But if it grows in an undisciplined way, will we not lose its tradition? Remember the image of Santa Claus, changed for the entire world by a soft drink company's promotional campaign. Should there not be concern about unchecked change?

Natural growth and development is different than change through distortion. This book has been written for a purpose. It does not elevate one method of practice over another. I offer instead to provide a traditional Japanese point of view based on actual experience. I believe it is important to know what the traditions are. In this way, while on your own path of practice, if you run into a situation that is difficult for you to understand, there is another point of view available to you. I hope this book serves as a useful part of your training.

Gaku Homma
May 1994
Denver, Colorado

I

内弟子編
Uchideshi Training

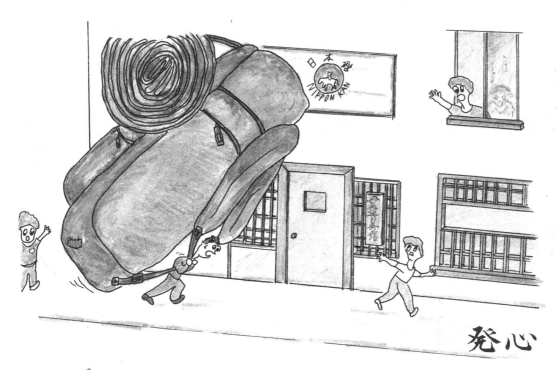

発心

1 *Hosshin*
(Deciding to Begin)

DECIDING TO BEGIN something is called *hosshin* in Japanese. All students, not only *uchideshi* candidates (those seeking training as live-in students) come to the *dojo* for the first time carrying with them a lot of expectations. This is like carrying an over-sized backpack full of dreams— expectations of how this new training will benefit them both physically and mentally. Usually new students who are the least familiar with Aikido bring the largest backpacks and have the most expectations.

If one is preparing for an unknown journey, there is no way to know if the path will lead to the ocean or to the mountains. Why, then, bring such cumbersome baggage? The door to the *dojo* is only three feet wide, so before an *uchideshi* candidate can enter, he or she must leave the backpack of expectations behind.

Once in a while, an *uchideshi* candidate stops by to visit the *dojo* for a few days to "check it out" before applying. This attitude is easily discerned in the way they approach their practice and other students. Being judgmental is not appropriate for beginning an *uchideshi* program. It is sincerely hoped that all candidates for *uchideshi* training achieve their goals, but sometimes the training is not really what a candidate is looking for. Especially for *yudansha* (students who hold a black belt degree) at another *dojo*, a letter of recommendation is required from their home *dojo*, out of respect for the student's instructors. Students who have practiced long enough to reach a black belt level in one *dojo* and wish to join an *uchideshi* program in another are sometimes having problems that need attention.

The reasons for deciding to seek *uchideshi* training vary from one individual to another. A hundred different candidates have a hundred different reasons for making that decision. No one questions their motives. *Uchideshi* training begins when one is able to detach themselves from the heavy baggage of dreams they carry. In other words, the training begins with discarding even one's own *hosshin*.

放置

2 *Hochi*
(Left Alone)

THIRTY TO FORTY Aikidoists a year contact Nippon Kan inquiring about *uchideshi* training. As a rule, all candidates for *uchideshi* training are welcomed, but this doesn't mean that they are all accepted. Whether one will be successful or not as an *uchideshi* depends upon his or her own efforts. Some come all prepared, physically that is, having packed their belongings, ready to move in. However, these hopefuls are not necessarily mentally prepared. Once an *uchideshi* candidate entered the practice area still wearing a portable radio. There have been others who tried bringing soft drink cans into the *dojo,* or entered chewing gum. Candidates like these don't usually stay very long.

If a candidate is found to be not quite ready for *uchideshi* training, a *dojo senpai* (senior student) may ask them to leave and come back when they are more ready to begin their training. In a rare unfortunate case, a candidate arrives only to be told that he is not ready for training after just putting his luggage down in the lobby. Most are permitted to stay overnight; however, this doesn't necessarily mean acceptance either. First the candidate must go through a trial period during which they are more or less left alone. A new candidate is shown to his or her room, told where the bathrooms are, and when practice is held. He or she is then left to themselves for a few days. This period serves to confirm one's resolution to become an *uchideshi*. For the senior office staff it provides an opportunity to see what kind of person the new candidate is, and how he or she interacts independently with other regular students.

Motives for wanting to become an *uchideshi* vary from one candidate to another. There are a few who blindly admire the status of a martial art *uchideshi* without really knowing what the training involves. Some consider it a way to escape from an unpleasant past or of avoiding the reality of their lives in the present. Some use an intention to become an *uchideshi* to impress family members or friends. Regardless of the candidate's motives, a few days of being left alone as they attend regular classes, although this may seem cold, will disclose their true motives and degree of determination. Applicants are requested to send in a résumé prior to their arrival, but it is impossible to evaluate someone just on paper. A personal evaluation is needed.

In order to help determine the applicants who will truly benefit from the program, this "left alone" period is set. Students who are really committed to go through the whole training program will be accepted at the end of this period.

自覚

3 Jikaku
(Self-Realization)

DURING THE *hochi* period, *uchideshi* candidates have many opportunities to watch the *senpai* in the *dojo,* and will often find the *senpai* cleaning. "Do you want me to help?" a candidate asks. "No, thank you," replies one of the *senpai.* The new *uchideshi* candidate cannot help but feel alienated. Being left alone without instruction on what to do or how to behave is a very difficult experience. Although this is a traditional Japanese approach which is somewhat foreign to average young American students, the methods of training in the *uchideshi* program each serve a purpose and are always meant to help the new *uchideshi* achieve their goals.

Alone again in his or her room, the *uchideshi* candidate contemplates the situation. "Why am I here?" "Why do I want to be an *uchideshi?*"

"Was I wrong to think I wanted this?" "This place is not what I expected." During this initial period of isolation, the *uchideshi* candidate faces himself and his doubts. He is still measuring his new environment with a ruler he brought from home. Even without any experience yet as an *uchideshi*, this young candidate judges what he sees, and this can cause him to have doubts.

The first thing a new *uchideshi* candidate must do to begin his or her training is to shed past opinions and judgments—they need to leave their egos behind. If this is not done, the new candidate enters training with a mind full of preconceptions. Their training will be filtered through what they expect to experience, not what the training actually is. This is likely to cause premature disappointment, and the student will not be able to accomplish his or her goals.

Therefore, until the initial excitement of arrival settles and the student regains the capacity to receive openly, the *uchideshi* candidate is left alone. If the candidate continues to speak about their past or their expectations for the future, the "left alone" period continues. During this period, the candidate must detach from dreams, expectations, and desires. This is the time to search for the true reason for seeking *uchideshi* training, and this time leads to self-realization.

策励

4 *Sakurei*
(Confirmation of Will)

USUALLY AFTER A few days, the *uchideshi* candidate will be interviewed by the *senpai*. At the meeting, stern-looking *senpai* surround him. After the days filled with unanswered questions, he doesn't quite know what to expect. Then the questioning begins. A *senpai* asks, "You have been spending a lot of time outside this *dojo* since you have arrived here. You have not done any of the tasks a student of this *dojo* should be doing. What are you thinking?" Another *senpai* asks, "You don't seem to have taken much initiative in learning or practicing. Do you really want to stay here for training?"

After first being left alone, the candidate must now answer questions like this. It does not seem to make any sense; however, this session is for the purpose of testing the candidate's determination to become a full-time *uchideshi*. If the candidate gets upset by the session, and begins accusing the *senpai* of not giving him proper attention or instruction, it would probably be the end of his chances of becoming an *uchideshi*.

This rather severe *sakurei* is a traditional form of initiation. In traditional Zen religious training, *saku* refers to an oak paddle used to administer a motivational whack to the shoulder of a monk in training. (The *"rei"* in *sakurei* means to "encourage or support.") By surviving this session a candidate becomes an *uchideshi* for at least one term. Always among the strict *senpai*, there will be one empathetic *senpai* who acts to help out the candidate when he does not know how to answer, or when he can't find the proper choice of words. "I know this candidate has been somewhat confused about his new environment, but he seems to have done what he thought was the best thing to do for the last few days. Why don't we let him continue to try?" offers the kindly *senpai*. The other *senpai* ask for assurance that the kind *senpai* who spoke up for the candidate will be responsible for the new *uchideshi's* behavior. To a candidate being interrogated, the kind *senpai* seems like a long lost friend, and from then on he will seek guidance from this person when he needs it.

The *senpai* who run the *dojo* office go through a very thorough evaluation of all *uchideshi* candidates and prescribe a detailed course of instruction for each one individually. Detailed instruction is given on how to take care of each *uchideshi* and the roles each *senpai* student will play in their development, based on the findings reported by the *senpai*. A kind *senpai* among stern ones is one such scenario. The objectives of an *uchideshi* are placed as a high priority, and many opportunities are provided through special training sessions to remind him of his goals. In traditional martial arts training, tough *sakurei* sessions are in a sense an expression of love.

5 *Jikatsu*
(Self-Reliance)

IF, UNFORTUNATELY, A candidate is denied acceptance as an *uchideshi* but still seeks training at the *dojo*, they may first need to find a place to live and means to support themselves. As explained earlier, when a candidate is not considered ready mentally to tackle *uchideshi* training, they must wait until they are ready. Until that time, they can continue their Aikido training as a commuting student.

There are a few who come to the *dojo* only posing as candidates for *uchideshi* training. In actuality, they are using the *dojo* as a temporary residence until they can find a job and a new home. For these few, it is tough not to be accepted because they are usually unprepared to look for another place to stay while trying to settle themselves. Although all students are welcome to practice at the *dojo*, it is not a rescue mission.

The operation of a *dojo* of over 250 students is costly, and all students have to contribute, including *uchideshi*. No one can afford to provide food and lodging for those not serious about the program.

"How did you intend to make ends meet without a penny?" a *senpai* scolds a new candidate. "First you must be able to support yourself before you can concentrate on your training." Being told this, the candidate must take the necessary steps toward self-reliance. He must find a place to live and work to support himself. While commuting to practice, he continues to seek training as an *uchideshi*. Even with candidates this determined, the *senpai* staff will watch them closely for a while and wait for a good time to accept them as a live-in *uchideshi*. This waiting period is also a part of training for serious candidates.

If a candidate is accepted as an *uchideshi,* he or she is asked to pay term fees in advance. The fee for the first three-month term at Nippon Kan is $900. The payment for the three-month term will not be refunded, even if the *uchideshi* decides to quit before completing the term. All *uchideshi* have to cook for themselves and pay for their own groceries. Usually the *uchideshi* pool their resources and cook meals together. Once an *uchideshi* completes his or her first term and moves on to the second term, the term fee is reduced to $750. For the third term, the fee is $600, and for the fourth term and thereafter, they pay $150 monthly per term. Special considerations may be made for students who are serious about their training and who continue to practice for a long time.

6 *Soji*
(Cleaning)

THE FIRST RESPONSIBILITY assigned a newly-admitted *uchideshi* is cleaning the *dojo*. No instruction is given on how to perform this task; they are told simply to "clean the *dojo*." Even though many new *uchideshi* have lived independently before coming to the *dojo*, it sometimes seems that all they know about cleaning is how to vacuum. Even if the new *uchideshi* is familiar with a vacuum cleaner, most do not know how to properly vacuum a *dojo* mat. Many long sheets of canvas are sewn together to cover the training space. Vacuuming at right angles over the seams can cause the mat to rip more easily. One cannot know this unless they have had experience in a *dojo* or have been told. Some new *uchideshi* vacuum as if they were mowing their backyard, moving back and forth from wall to wall. If a *senpai* were to see this, he would scold, "You can't vacuum that way! Don't just push the vacuum in a straight line. You're just stirring up dust. Push forward and back as you move sideways. Think of it as the rowing exercise we practice in each class." As the new *uchideshi* continues cleaning, another *senpai* appears to check the corners and the floor. After wiping his finger on a cleaned surface he inquires, "Did you really clean here?" The new *uchideshi* rushes over with a bucket full of water and a rag and starts washing the surface again, forgetting to rinse the rag. The *senpai* offers some stern advice: "Rinse the rag before you wipe, or you'll only get the place more dirty!" Another *uchideshi* starts to help but begins dusting after the mat has been vacuumed and the floors washed. *Senpai* again offers some advice, "Do you put on your shoes before putting on your underwear? There is a logical order to follow!" If the cleaning supplies are not neatly put away in the closet, a *senpai* will call a meeting of the *uchideshi* concerned—even pulling them out of practice to point out the problem. In telling them what *not* to do, it is unlikely that the *senpai* will tell them how to do it. "Don't ask me how to wash your own face!" chides the *senpai*.

This probably sounds a little harsh, but there is a reason behind it. Part of *uchideshi* training is learning to work out each task on one's own—to find one's own way to accomplish duties. This is much more important than developing individuals who cannot do anything unless they are told how to, step by step.

The purpose of *soji* is not only to remove dust from the *dojo*. The process of cleaning itself is considered a part of training. If a new *uchideshi* thinks that there is no important reason for cleaning the *dojo*, the *senpai* will be ready with another lesson for them to learn.

7 *Nichiji Kanri* (Managing Daily Chores)

SINCE THE *dojo* space is rather large, cleaning is a major task. Normally, basic tidying-up is done prior to class by all students, but there may not be enough time to do a thorough cleaning just before class begins. Besides, taking care of the *dojo* is not limited only to cleaning. Plants need to be watered regularly, towels and toilet paper replaced often, and supplies organized. Each *uchideshi* must keep a list of chores to be done in their head at all times. Especially during periods when there are less *uchideshi* living at the *dojo*, each has a lot more to do to keep the *dojo* running smoothly. By performing these daily tasks, the *uchideshi* develop a good sense of how to manage responsibilities in their own lives.

A student's ability to organize his or her time and actions is evident on the mat during practice. When an *uchideshi* does only what he or she is told to do in performing their daily chores, their practice on the mat also tends to be passive. Being excessively passive does not always bring about positive growth. Until new *uchideshi* can take their own initiative in managing daily chores, *senpai* will be after them. A new *uchideshi* might think, "I didn't come here just to learn how to clean," but if someone cannot handle cleaning the *dojo,* they will not be successful in the larger aspects of their training.

Those who succeed in this kind of *uchideshi* training are the ones who will sweep away a few fallen leaves in autumn knowing that there will be only more to follow the very next day, without complaint.

Washing the floor with a wet rag is in fact very good exercise. By including it in their training, the new *uchideshi* begin their journey. This is a very important first step, learning how to organize time and manage daily chores.

8 *Jisui*
(Cooking for Yourself)

"Ummm, one cup of what? Oh, no ... first I have to go buy a measuring cup!" It is rare for new *uchideshi* to know how to cook; the majority don't really even know how to hold a cooking knife properly.

"Ever since you came here, you have been eating out or buying frozen dinners. You cannot learn to take care of yourself this way. From now on you need to learn to cook for yourself." The *uchideshi* remembers *senpai's* lecture from the day before. Shortly after being told to begin cooking for themselves, the refrigerator appears filled with fresh groceries. Unfortunately, in the beginning most of it spoils before it is used. When this sort of waste is pointed out by the *senpai*, canned foods and frozen dinners start appearing again.

An important part of *uchideshi* training is learning to maintain one's health. Eating balanced foods that meet the physical requirements of training is essential. Eating out in restaurants is not only expensive, it takes away the opportunity to learn to prepare balanced meals that satisfy the body's needs while training. To encourage this development, the new *uchideshi* are instructed to stay away from restaurants and frozen foods.

On the door of the *dojo* refrigerator there is a sign that says, "Use of the kitchen by all *uchideshi* will be prohibited if food is found spoiled in the refrigerator." Making the best use of basic foods teaches respect and encourages us to give new life to simple ingredients. Foods are meant to give life, to be put to good use by those preparing them. There is nothing more difficult than learning to do this. Over and over, the *uchideshi* are coached and scolded by the *senpai* as they try to learn how to cook for themselves. Learning how to divide groceries into single-sized portions, choosing what will be used for the next morning and evening meal, freezing what will not used, and repackaging leftovers are all skills to be mastered.

Learning to cultivate a mind that thinks in terms of efficient management helps develop a caring heart for all that is provided to us. This in turn leads to love and appreciation for oneself and others. The new *uchideshi* try to follow cookbooks, rather seriously—only to find that it is not such an easy task.

居室管理

9 *Ishitsu Kanri*
(Keeping Orderly Quarters)

WITHOUT NOTICE, THE *uchideshi* are informed that the *senpai* are conducting a room inspection. The *senpai* make their way into the living quarters, leaving no time to straighten up.

The privacy of each *uchideshi* is fully respected, but an inspection is a different matter. As long as they are living in the *dojo* as *uchideshi*, they are in training twenty-four hours a day, seven days a week. Even when sleeping, it is best not to forget that one is in training.

The living quarters are the only place in the *dojo* where an *uchideshi* can sometimes relax, or be alone to do some inward searching. Such an important space must be kept clean and neat. Even when the rest of the *dojo* is clean and spotless, it is not time to rest. Everything in the *uchideshi's* room must be neatly put away. Anything that has no use should be disposed of. Pictures on the wall must be hanging straight, flower vases standing tall, plants sufficiently watered. It is natural to want to keep things in good order, but many times people get used to a disordered environment. Where the *uchideshi* live, it is vital that everything be in order. If it is not, how can they concentrate on their training?

If one thinks that crooked pictures and wilted plants have no bearing on training, there might be a need to reevaluate being an *uchideshi*. Are *uchideshi* not trying to establish internal order in themselves? If someone cannot maintain a visible order in their environment, it will certainly be difficult to develop a natural and healthy order in their minds—which is not as visible.

Once, an *uchideshi* was discovered meditating in his room with his belongings scattered around him. Firmly, the *senpai* told him, "Stop being lazy. I know why you just sit there and meditate. Your belongings are strewn everywhere and you want to cover them up by sitting on them. Don't waste time, start cleaning!"

People who meditate in dumpsters won't find what they seek.

10 *Sentaku*
(Laundry)

A DOG FOLLOWS, SNIFFING. Another small dog some distance away barks frantically. "Thanks to you both, everyone is now staring at me. What do they think I am?" laments a red-faced new *uchideshi* on his way to do laundry.

Living as an *uchideshi* without much money, one is forced to lead a very frugal life. Pinching here and there, saving as much as possible, the *uchideshi* conduct their daily lives. When it comes to doing laundry, this *uchideshi* waits until it is absolutely necessary. Cleaning is not an appropriate description for his actions—he is simply trying to reduce the annoying smell of sweat on his clothes. To save a few cents he tries to put as much laundry as he can fit into the washing machine.

Many *uchideshi* come from out-of-state and do not have a car. This means they have to put their clothes in duffel bags and carry them to a nearby laundromat. Nippon Kan is equipped with a large kitchen and jacuzzi bath, but there is no washer or dryer. This is not for financial reasons. The decision not to install a laundry facility is based on the basic principle that besides training uniforms (*keiko-gi*), an *uchideshi* does not have great need for a large wardrobe. Of course everyone needs a few changes of clothes and underwear, but these can be washed in the janitor's sink. Uniforms can be washed in the shower and hung outside to dry. In Colorado, it often doesn't even take a whole day to dry clothes in the open air. During their first weeks of training, many *uchideshi* try washing their own clothes and uniforms in the sink and shower, but as the pile of clothes grows larger, the walk to the laundromat begins to seem more appealing.

Uchideshi training can be compared to doing laundry. If you do not wash your clothes, they begin to smell, and there are less clean clothes left to wear. If you do not make yourself shiny with daily training, you become dull and lose awareness of yourself—even to the point that one day you might need help from somebody else.

On the way to the laundromat the *uchideshi* attracts whistles and shouts from a group of teenagers in a passing sports car. Even doing laundry is considered part of training.

11

Shokuji Settai
(Serving Meals)

As SOON AS the last evening class is over, the *uchideshi* run to the kitchen and begin to prepare for dinner. In the *dojo*, evening meals are cooked for *senpai* who stay after class, or for special guests.

Preparing dinner is one of the *uchideshi's* many tasks. Dinner tonight for the *senpai* is a large pot of soup filled with all sorts of fresh ingredients. This meal only takes about a half-hour to prepare. Not only is it easy, it also tastes very good. In learning to make this simple meal, the *uchideshi* learn many basics in food preparation, from peeling and cutting vegetables to boning chicken. In the beginning, after watching an *uchideshi* struggle for a while with these tasks, a *senpai* remarks, "You are working so slowly the potatoes are going to sprout, and that chicken will start breathing again! You are cooking dinner, not tomorrow's breakfast." With that the *senpai* takes over in the kitchen and starts cooking with amazing efficiency. The *uchideshi* can learn from watching the *senpai,* but there are no verbal instructions given.

By the time the main dish is ready, a portable grill has been set up at a large table, and rice bowls, soup bowls, and chopsticks must be properly arranged. With so many things to coordinate, there is no time to just watch the food cook without performing other tasks. For guests who like to drink hot *saké* (rice wine), water needs to be heated to make it hot, and *saké* cups must be readied. For the others, glasses need to be set out. Everything needs to be ready and in perfect order when dinner is served.

The *uchideshi* don't eat until all the *senpai* and guests have finished their meal. One *uchideshi* is assigned to wait on the table to make sure the rice bowls are kept full. There is a proper way to accomplish even such a small task as refilling a rice bowl. One has to know how to hold the rice bowl, how much rice to put in, and how to offer a filled rice bowl to a guest. The only time a rice bowl is filled completely to the brim is during ceremonial offerings to the deceased in Japan. If an *uchideshi* were to serve a bowl full of heaping rice, a *senpai* might respond with, "Don't fill the bowl so much. I'm not quite dead yet!"

"Don't put your finger in the bowl!" "Can we get some tea?" "What?! We are out of hot water?" Remembering very well their early days as *uchideshi* students, the *senpai* never seem to find an end to the mistakes made by the new *uchideshi*.

食器洗い

12

Shokki Arai
(Washing Dishes)

THE PARTY IS almost over and most of the guests and *senpai* have gone home. The *dojo* is empty except for a few remaining *senpai* who are emptying a few more beer cans for the trash. It is very close to midnight, and it is time for the *uchideshi* to start cleaning up. Often the *uchideshi* have missed grabbing something to eat for themselves, being too busy looking after guests and *senpai*. Now it is time to use any remaining soup and cook some rice to make their own dinner. Left-over soup is very tasty, since the vegetables and meats have been simmering for a long time.

It is not uncommon for sixty or seventy people to take part in a *dojo* party. Food preparation begins a few days prior, and the guests receive the best hospitality possible during dinner. The *uchideshi's* hard work does not end after all the happy guests have gone home. For a formal party, paper plates or cups are not used; so, after such a dinner many dishes and plates must be washed. A full-course dinner party is rather lavish, and for the *uchideshi* who have been eating their own cooking, the uneaten left-overs that come back to the kitchen are quite attractive. Checking to be sure that dishes are untouched, the *uchideshi* put them aside to enjoy after clean-up is finished. In the meantime, the dishes are washed and put away neatly.

Preparing for dinner, setting tables, serving food and drinks, cleaning up and washing dishes — one task follows another until everything is done. By the time the *uchideshi* can retire to their rooms, it is well past two o' clock in the morning. These events are especially hard for the *uchideshi* who have regular jobs to go to early the next morning. But be sure to remember that those *senpai* who stayed late enjoying the feast went through the very same training that new *uchideshi* are going through now.

総活

13 *Soukatsu* (Critique Therapy)

PRESSED BY THE busy schedule of *uchideshi* life, training, cleaning, doing laundry, preparing meals, and helping host parties, two months may fly by before an *uchideshi* becomes aware of the passing time. All *uchideshi* are expected to attend at least two Aikido classes a day, and their schedule is made even more difficult if they also hold down regular jobs.

One night, after regular classes have finished for the evening and all the commuting students have left, an *uchideshi* finds himself surrounded by *senpai* in a corner of the *dojo*. It is a *soukatsu* session, in which the *senpai* ask questions and critique a new *uchideshi's* performance. The purpose of this session is to review the last few months of the *uchideshi's* training, summarize his or her accomplishments, and point out the areas he or she still needs to work on.

Placed in the middle of a circle of stern-faced *senpai* standing with arms folded, the session proceeds with questions followed by criticism. This *uchideshi's* cleaning of the *dojo* has not been thoroughly done. His attitude during dinner parties has been unacceptable, dishes were rather poorly washed. The kitchen was left a mess after preparing a meal. The *senpai* come up with a number of criticisms, and ask the *uchideshi* to explain his behavior. Even the *senpai* who previously had stood up for the *uchideshi* joins in. "I hate to mention it, because I'm supposed to be looking after your training, but. . . ." And he lists a few tasks that the *uchideshi* had not been doing properly. One of the more severe *senpai* offers: "When one person does not pull his weight around here, there is much more for the rest to attend to. Maybe it is time for this *uchideshi* to end his training."

For the *uchideshi* subjected to this interrogation and criticism, it is a rather upsetting session. "I'm doing my best, and I'm doing a lot for the *dojo*. What these *senpai* are saying is not reasonable at all," he laments.

Soukatsu sessions are conducted under specific direction. The office staff monitors closely each *uchideshi*, continually reevaluating his or her development. What each *uchideshi* needs as his or her training progresses is discussed often in the office, and different levels of instruction are given according to the *uchideshi's* development. After a few months of training, an *uchideshi* may begin to feel comfortable with the program and with other students at the *dojo*, and he may forget that his position is much different from the other students who attend classes on a more casual basis. A *soukatsu* session is scheduled in order to bring this awareness back to his attention. The *senpai* who surrounded the *uchideshi* on this occasion have all been through similar *soukatsu* sessions when they were new to their training. These sessions are held with the intention of helping *uchideshi* accomplish their goals.

見取稽古

14 *Mitori Geiko*
(Practice Through Observation)

DURING THE FIRST month, a new *uchideshi* is required to observe black belt and expert classes twice a week. After this initial observation period, an *uchideshi* is allowed to participate in these advanced level classes. By observing and later practicing in these classes, the new *uchideshi* learns a lot about basic techniques, how these techniques lead to more advanced techniques, and even more about serious practice etiquette. This is called *mitori geiko,* "practice through observation."*

---

*The word *keiko* ("practice"), when preceded by another qualifying proverb, becomes *geiko.*

"You have been asked to come and observe black belt class." At first, the new *uchideshi* is very excited. However, observing a class is not like watching a movie, and he soon finds it is not easy to just sit and observe for a long period of time. While instruction is given, all students sit in *seiza* (formal kneeling position) to listen, and the *uchideshi* are expected to sit in the same fashion. After instruction is given, while the students are practicing, the *uchideshi* watching the class are allowed to sit cross-legged in a more relaxed manner. There have been *uchideshi* who are used to sitting in *seiza*, and a new *uchideshi* may feel compelled to try to follow suit. After a few minutes of sitting in *seiza*, one of the new *uchideshi* casually leans forward as if *really* interested in the black belt practice going on in front of him. Actually, this is a good way to get the blood flowing back into feet which are becoming numb from lack of circulation.

After a few more minutes of watching, the *uchideshi* begins to feel that it would have been much easier to be out there on the mat being thrown about by the *senpai* than trying to sit still and watch class sitting in *seiza*. Watching the clock gradually becomes more important. The minute hands slow down to a crawl. Another regular student watches the class from a chair, due to a twisted ankle he suffered in a mountain climbing accident. The *uchideshi* eyes him enviously, almost wishing he too had a sprained ankle so he could sit in a chair!

After class is finally finished, the *uchideshi* tries to rise, but his feet are completely numb. He discovers that he is not really able to walk just quite yet. The *senpai* tease good naturedly, "What happened to you? Are you feeling ill? Was our practice so hard that you are too exhausted to get up?" Even as they tease, the *senpai* know exactly what the *uchideshi* is going through and remember their own experiences well.

産合氣

自主稽古

15 *Jishu Geiko*
(Solitary Practice)

OUTSIDE REGULAR CLASS hours, *uchideshi* are required to practice on their own for at least one hour a day. Each picks a time that works best with their schedule. Each student reports on their practice to the office daily. The new *uchideshi's* frame of mind is being prepared gradually to focus more seriously on their training. During the first few hectic weeks, the *uchideshi's* life has been busy learning how to cook and clean, and an occasional *soukatsu* session has left him slightly confused, with mixed expectations. By now he is ready to concentrate on training with a new outlook. The office staff keeps a close eye on all *uchideshi,* who are usually not aware that they are being so closely observed. In some cases it is easy to predict when and for what reasons a certain *uchideshi* will decide to give up their training.

A new *uchideshi* is given chores and tasks and is left more or less to themselves in order for them to develop a mind open to this new experience without judging it by their past.

There is a well-known story in Japan of a young *unsui* (priest in training) who applied to study under a famous *Roshi*. The *Roshi* ordered the *unsui* to fill his bath with water from the well and gave him a bucket with no bottom with which to perform the task. The *unsui* did as he was asked and filled the bath, although it was a very slow and tedious task with a bottomless bucket. In the *Roshi's* mind if the *unsui* had questioned the validity of this request, he would not have been ready to pursue serious training.

Practicing alone in an unheated *dojo* during the coldest part of winter, we hear only the sound of the *uchideshi's* breathing and the shuffling of his feet. Occasionally, you can hear him tapping his body with his fists to remind himself to concentrate. When he has completed his targeted number of exercise repetitions, he shouts out in triumph. He is in training for himself, not for anybody else. Simply training for the purpose of training is the next step for the true *uchideshi*. This alone will give him the foundation for all his Aikido training to come.

16 *Keiko*
(Practice)

ONE OF THE prerogatives of being an *uchideshi* is to be able to participate in black belt classes, or any other special classes, even if he or she is a white belt ranked student. Practicing among much more advanced students and trying to keep up with them is not an easy task. The first trick an *uchideshi* learns is how to tie his belt loosely so that it comes undone every so often. In this way he can take a short break to catch his breath while he is tying his belt again. Of course, all *senpai* students know this trick and will not give a new *uchideshi* a chance to rest even with an untied belt. In this case the clever *uchideshi* has to continue his practice with his uniform flapping awkwardly about him.

Keiko (practice) is the highest priority for an *uchideshi*, and no matter how busy he or she is with other tasks, he or she must attend classes daily. Those who hold down day jobs or work nights need to make sure that there is absolutely no conflict between their jobs and practice schedule. *Keiko* for the *uchideshi* is not a spare-time activity, second in importance to their job. Rather, jobs are held down in an *uchideshi's* spare time to support their training at the *dojo*.

At first, an enthusiastic *uchideshi* tries to attend all of the classes held each day. At Nippon Kan there are three classes held over a four-hour period each evening. When considering this training as a long-term program, it is better to not push too hard or too fast. Pacing is a very important part of planning. It is better to try to attend two classes each evening. Basically, an *uchideshi* is in training twenty-four hours a day, and although practice is the highest priority, it is important to try and maintain some balance.

The lessons to be learned at the *dojo* are not always taught only on the mat. It has been found that overly-enthusiastic new *uchideshi* who practice at all classes tend to try to stockpile new techniques while ignoring the other aspects of their training. In such cases it is better for them to be told to reduce the number of classes they attend. Concentrating excessively on classes may produce a skillful Aikido technician, but there is much more than technique to be learned. A balance of activities is important for overall development. Towards this end, ten minutes of toilet cleaning can be equal in worth to an hour of practice in class.

稽古三昧

17 *Keiko Zanmai*
(Just Practice)

"I T LOOKS LIKE I am not going to get much use out of this dress—and to think I brought it all the way from Japan." There are many social events and parties at the *dojo*, but for all *uchideshi*, parties are a time spent busily cleaning, preparing, serving, and tidying up.

Traditionally in Japan, *dojos* have been a place of training for men, and it is important that the women who join this program understand this. Students who join the *uchideshi* program are most often men, but some women have joined in the past. *Uchideshi* life in general has many rules that may be hard for American students to understand. At this *dojo*, a special program specifically geared toward women does not exist. Women are accepted like their male counterparts on a case-by-case basis, and no special allowances are made for anyone.

"Jeans well-patched at the knees and faded sweatshirts are the closest I will get to dressing up here!" During the cold winter months layer upon layer of sweaters are worn by all the *uchideshi*, making everyone look like odd-shaped mounds waddling around while waiting for the arrival of spring. Cosmetics are definitely not needed, although lotion is helpful for hands rough from *bokken* (wooden sword) practice and washing dishes.

"I wonder how much money I spent in the years I lived in Tokyo. All those clothes and gourmet foods I used to buy . . . anything I wanted. After living here, the past seems so different. Who was I back then? Looking at the letters and photos from my friends back home, it all seems somewhat frivolous and unimportant now."

These are the words of a young lady from Tokyo, who learned much about life and herself in the year she spent in the *uchideshi* program.

The point of concentration in the life of the *uchideshi* is: *keiko, keiko, keiko.* This is *keiko zanmai.*

苦脳

18 *Kuno* (The Struggle)

ONCE IN A while, an *uchideshi* leaves the *dojo*, seen off only by Nippon Kan's dog Ponk. Usually it is very early in the morning or late at night.

When a hundred people gather, it is for a hundred different reasons. As I have said before, when an *uchideshi* is admitted to the program, they are not asked their reasons for joining. His or her past or ultimate future prospects are not as much of a concern as their present state of mind and body. What is more important for an *uchideshi* is to give their best effort today ... now.

If this training is chosen as an escape from the past, an *uchideshi* may still put forth an impressive display of sincerity and commitment. However, it may be the same as a convicted criminal shaving his head to demonstrate that he has changed his ways—merely a facade. If it is a facade, "metal plating easily wears off," as the saying goes. The *uchideshi* with a change of heart will start looking for justifiable excuses to stop their training.

Originally they might have just been rebelling against parents, or trying to get over being abandoned by a loved one. At the time, they felt strongly enough about their convictions to join the program. But as time passes and wounds heal, the importance of this decision can be forgotten. Some students decide they want to return to their other life. When this kind of change takes place inside themselves, some *uchideshi* begin to criticize the program in order to justify their change of heart. They need to find a valid reason for leaving their training without completing the program. "This place is too Japanese. I am an American and this is America!" one student exclaimed as he left the program. This same student had previously complained, "America today is not right. Something is very wrong in this country today." By leaving, these *uchideshi* will have to live with the weight of another disappointment.

If an *uchideshi* develops a negative attitude about their training and the program, there are no kind words offered to comfort them. No one stops them if they gesture to leave. This holds true for all students, not only the *uchideshi*.

Do (the way) is both coming and going. Arriving is one way, and leaving is another. The direction that you face is always in front of you. Wherever you are headed, I wish you good luck.

19 *Gakushu*
(Studying)

IN A CORNER of his chilly living quarters, an *uchideshi* sits hunched over his desk until the wee hours of the morning. As well as being an *uchideshi,* he is a full-time college student. Trying to achieve both of these goals at the same time is a worthy challenge. We are all given a life to live. No matter what we do with it, just living it day by day each second is hardly a waste, since living is in itself quite wonderful. But part of the joy life can offer us is in the challenge of searching for the true path each of us needs to find and follow. Those who use their time while they are young in this pursuit are well worthy of respect.

Even to most Japanese people today, having the experience of living in a traditional Japanese *dojo* is unique. For someone to undergo this training, pursue his academic studies, and even hold down a part-time job, all at the same time, is very difficult. Surviving the experience will make a very unique kind of individual, one who holds the world in his hands.

In the spring of 1993, one of our *uchideshi* graduated from college with honors and simultaneously completed four terms of *uchideshi* training. He went on to teach English for one year at the Nippon Kan cultural exchange center in Naruse Village in Akita Prefecture, Japan.

20 *Yojo*
(Taking Care)

"I WANT TO go home!" "What are you talking about? Shape up, you only have a cold." "But I've never felt like this!" "In Japan we say only fools and monkeys don't catch colds ... all you need is a little rest."

For an *uchideshi* the hardest training of all is when he is not able to practice. Staying in your room while everyone else is practicing is no fun. There have even been times when an under-the-weather *uchideshi* has been caught sneaking out of his room, just to watch others practice.

Having taken on the challenge of training, most new *uchideshi* think they are impervious to any illness or accident. If a cold does set in or they suffer a minor sprain or strain, panic ensues. It is an important rule of training to avoid injuring oneself or a partner, but practicing every day leads to an occasional minor bump or bruise.

When an *uchideshi* can't practice, this is a chance to reflect on the value of one's health. It is an opportunity to experience how vulnerable human bodies can be, and how important being healthy is. Being patient during times of illness teaches us a lot about taking care of ourselves.

If an *uchideshi* becomes ill he is exempt from all of the normal tasks and training schedules he usually follows until he is feeling better. He is taken care of, and left to rest and concentrate on taking care of himself. In such a time, he realizes the kindness of fellow students and staff who tend to his needs with warmth and kindness.

21 *Hata Samu*
(Working in the Vegetable Garden)

SEEDS THAT HAVE been planted begin to sprout. The *uchideshi* tries to distinguish the leaves of the new vegetables from those of weeds. If he grew up in the city, or has been accustomed to finding vegetables only in grocery stores, this is not an easy task. Often new vegetable sprouts are pulled, mistaken for weeds. Once a certain *uchideshi* was told to pull carrots and daikon radishes, and he enthusiastically answered, "OK!" and took off to the garden. Interestingly enough, he did not return soon. It later became known that he didn't know what carrots and daikon radishes looked like above the ground. He knew what they looked like, but only as produce in the grocery store.

At times when questions and uncertainty about *uchideshi* life seem to be occupying a lot of his thoughts, working in the garden offers a welcome opportunity for reflection. Thinking back about life so far at the *dojo*, this *uchideshi* realizes that most of his memories are of being ordered about by the *senpai*, cleaning the *dojo*, washing dishes, and many other endless chores. Hours of hard training on the mat also comes to mind. It might be easy for him to conclude that the program does not really have a lot of benefits. Interestingly though, while most *uchideshi* show noticeable improvement and grow steadily, they may not realize the change taking place in them.

Carrots and radishes sprout from seeds and endure the heat, cold, rain, and wind as they struggle to grow. We can compare this to ourselves. People are like carrots and radishes, sometimes unable to see the growth in themselves.

If you open a seed and look inside, there are no vegetables to be seen. Yet, without seeds, the soil cannot produce vegetables. To grow a vegetable from a seed, it takes continuous attention, care, and the blessings of nature. Working in the vegetable garden gives the *uchideshi* the chance to witness this growth first-hand. We need to be aware of this wonderful mystery, and putting our hands in the soil is a way to do just that.

親愛

22 *Shinai*
(Parents' Love)

A PACKAGE ARRIVES a few days before Christmas from home. Inside the package is a long letter from Mom, a warm sweater, gloves, and Christmas cookies. The hardships that an *uchideshi* goes through, evidenced by rough and blistered hands from constant practice with the *bokken*, are softened by a small package filled with love from his family.

Boarding conditions at the *dojo* are tough regardless of the season. In winter, a small enclosed oil heater is placed in each room, for Nippon Kan has no central heating system. An air-conditioner was recently installed for the hot summer months, but it is only used from 5:00 P.M. to 9:00 P.M. to cool down the rooms before bedtime. As a general rule, the heater is turned on in the winter when the plants in the lobby begin to freeze, and only for about one hour a day before classes begin. Once practice starts, the space is heated by the rigorous movement of human bodies.

Being cold in the winter and hot in the summer is natural, and when one learns to live with these conditions, one can overcome suffering from hot and cold. Alignment is a much different form of conquering. When it is hot, it is hot; and when it is cold, it is cold. What is important here is to learn to accept and live with such conditions.

In winter, the *dojo* windows are covered with plastic sheets, to seal all openings that let in cold air. The *uchideshi* wear heavy jackets, even inside, and heavy socks to help protect them from the cold. In summer, fans from the pawnshop help to bring in cool air from the outside after sunset. It is important to experience the seasons with the whole body. There is no use complaining about the *dojo* being too cold or too hot. The *dojo* exists here in its natural condition.

An old man in a snow-covered mountain village waits silently for spring. At the same time another man leads his camel through the blistering desert. Both realize the truth in their surroundings and learn to accept it. This is truly joining with nature, and it leads to absolute strength.

In the middle of the coldest part of winter, the *uchideshi* learns to appreciate the love his parents sent with a jar of cookies. He brings the jar to me to share, saying, "These are from my mom." No matter how old one becomes, one is blessed by the love of parents.

裏方

23 Urakata
(Helpers Behind the Scenes)

IF AN *uchideshi* makes it through one term without major problems, he owes a lot to the doings of the *urakata*. The *urakata* do not wear special uniforms, so they are not easily identified. The *urakata* never disclose that they are in fact the ones helping the *uchideshi* as they pass through their many obstacles and complete their numerous duties. In most cases, an *uchideshi* does not even realize that he or she is being helped by the *urakata*. Initiation and group critique sessions take place under the guidance of the *urakata* who are closely watching the *uchideshi*. Many *uchideshi* go through similar stages at a similar pace within the first three months. Sometimes they feel rejected and lose sight of their goals; sometimes they become confused or frustrated, what we in general call the *"uchideshi* syndrome." The *urakata* are most effective at times like these.

Well into the third month of training, the *uchideshi* begin to work with some of the *urakata*. When the *dojo* is planning for the arrival of a new *uchideshi*, the *urakata* and *uchideshi* work together to make things ready. They busily clean up the living quarters for the new arrival, making the bed and setting out extra sheets and towels. The room is decorated with flowers, and a guide to Denver is placed on the table. It is not until now that the *uchideshi* realizes what pains were taken to prepare for his own arrival, as he works on preparations for the newest *uchideshi*. This discovery renews the *uchideshi's* appreciation for the *urakata*. Thinking back over the last few month spent at the *dojo,* he realizes that the *urakata* and the *senpai* always knew exactly what he had been going through. They knew when he was frustrated or felt overwhelmed by doubts, as if he was under their control at all times. It is a humbling moment.

The *urakata* work efficiently without many words. Their actions reflect their state-of-mind and are not done for benefiting themselves or reaping rewards from others. Humbly thinking of how he had been helped and guided by the *urakata*, a young *uchideshi* left a note upon his completion of one year's training: "It is time now for me to step off the palm of their guiding hands." In June 1991, this *uchideshi* returned to Japan at the age of twenty-three.

雑務管理

24 *Zatsumu Kanri* (Managing Various Duties)

"OH, NO! SOMEBODY, please bring me a roll of toilet paper!" Once in a while, this sort of thing happens in the men's *uchideshi* living quarters. It is not taken lightly if a *senpai* or commuting student finds themselves in this predicament. A meeting would be organized immediately after class, and the lack of attention to managing daily supplies would be strongly pointed out.

By the end of the first term, it is likely that a more seasoned *uchideshi* would be sharing chores and duties with a newer *uchideshi*. Up until now, it was not even thinkable to enter the administration office. But today he is told that from now on he will be responsible for *dojo* maintenance and office supplies. He has become part of the *dojo* operations team. This is a time for the *uchideshi* to feel proud. Of course, managing maintenance and office supplies is not an easy task. He has to check the inventory of janitorial supplies, maintain equipment and tools used for seminars and classes, and make sure that the office does not run out of pens, stamps, and other necessities. When a *senpai* asks, "Where are the stamps?" the *uchideshi* in charge heads for the door to buy more stamps as quickly as possible. It is not good for the error to be discovered by a *senpai* trying to complete important office matters.

To maintain the supply inventory, the *uchideshi* in charge is given $50.00 as a petty cash fund. Part of his job includes keeping a ledgered account of all expenses. In this way the *uchideshi* gradually learns to help run an office smoothly and efficiently.

Nippon Kan is a Federal nonprofit organization and for the past fifteen years the training fees for regular members has been kept at thirty dollars per month. In other words, thirty times the number of students enrolled is the monthly revenue. The more students there are, the more revenue is generated, but the expenses also run higher. To manage the budget, it is important to eliminate excessive or wasteful expenditures. The best way to reduce waste is efficient management of supplies. It isn't long before an *uchideshi* becomes aware of the difficulties of *dojo* management and the reasons why strict rules are applied to its operations.

25 *Jisha*
(The Attendant)

AFTER ABOUT AN hour into a hike an *uchideshi* remarks, "Nice scenery isn't it, *Sensei?*" obviously wanting to rest a bit. "Yes indeed," I reply and continue walking.

When I go out or need to work on a project at the *dojo*, I often call on an *uchideshi*, or sometimes two, to accompany or assist me. Especially close to the end of a term, an *uchideshi* often receives this honor. The event could be my private business or a meal. On weekends in the spring, summer and fall, I often go hiking. In winter, I sometimes take an *uchideshi* skiing. You may think that the life of the *uchideshi* is not that tough after all, providing all sorts of opportunities to enjoy the Rocky Mountains. That is not quite true, if one looks at it from the *uchideshi's* point of view. Many *uchideshi* come from out-of-state. As you know, Denver is known as the "Mile High City" and the air is very thin. Hiking at high altitude in the mountains for six hours in one day is very physically challenging. Hiking in the Rockies for the first time, you usually have quite a time trying to keep up with the people in front of you. On top of being physically exerting, comments from the *senpai* like "Strength in your legs and lower back is very important in the martial arts. Have you been neglecting your training?" make it that much harder to keep up.

I believe that anyone who teaches martial arts must be a good example both inside and outside the *dojo*. For this reason I often invite *uchideshi* who are close to finishing a term, so that they have more chances to learn outside the *dojo*. Despite my intentions, there are some who mistake this invitation as a sign of favoritism, and begin to act overly friendly and casual. Even though they are nearing the completion of a term, this is not the time to relax or forget one's place. More than ever, it is a time for evaluation and testing—testing directly by the chief instructor.

Accomplishment means ascending a peak, but it does not mean that one will stay there. What's left after reaching the top of a peak is the climb down. If an *uchideshi* tries to stay at the top, he will soon be escorted once again to the bottom.

寒中鍛練

26 *Kanchu Tanren*
(Training in the Cold)

SPECIAL OUTDOOR TRAINING during the summer consists of hiking and jogging. For those who begin their *uchideshi* training during the winter months, there are special training sessions held during January and February, when the weather is coldest.

When regular classes have finished at nine o'clock in the evening, the *uchideshi* are called back to the practice area, instructed to wear only the pants of their *keiko-gi* (training uniform) and a belt. First they practice *shikofumi* (lifting one leg high to the side and swinging it down pushing hard on the floor). This exercise is repeated on both sides many times. *Shikofumi* is followed by a few sets of push-ups. After everyone has warmed up, sumo wrestling is practiced. Steam starts to rise from hard-working bodies.

When everyone is fully warmed-up, *ukemi* practice (falling from throws) begins. After only a short while, the coldness of the mat feels nice on sweaty skin. After a week of this training, running barefoot outside is added to the late night session. After finally getting used to this, a cold shower in front of the *dojo* upon the return from the run is added to complete *Kanchu Tanren*. At first, when the *uchideshi* hears that they are to run outside barefoot, gasps of astonishment can be heard. "Careful not to slip or fall," I say, leading the way. I take the first splash of cold water, then the *uchideshi* follow. Under these conditions, the water feels warm to the senses.

Water during summer training is refreshing and pleasant, but water in winter is cold. It is naturally so. The same water feels different depending on one's circumstances. It is up to each individual *uchideshi* to interpret the training as pleasant or unpleasant. Only after positioning oneself in very strenuous conditions and withstanding it, can one feel the warmth of cold water in winter and truly appreciate it. A splash of cold water is a hint from the *senpai* and the *urakata* from which the *uchideshi* may learn. Its purpose is not to boost the ego, but simply to help one reach self-awareness.

Training is, after all, repetition of these stages of awareness.

無礼講

27 *Bureiko*
(A Party for Blowing Off Steam)

THE LIFE OF the *uchideshi* is rigorous, demanding complete dedication. Some *uchideshi* hold down regular jobs outside the *dojo* during the day or late in the evening after classes have finished. On top of their outside responsibilities, there are *dojo* duties and chores which must not be neglected. Of course, attending classes is a top priority. During the weekdays, three regular classes are scheduled from five o'clock until nine o'clock in the evening. All *uchideshi* are required to attend two classes every weekday evening, and to practice on their own when regular classes are not in session.

Obviously, an *uchideshi's* life is quite busy during the week. After morning class on the weekends is often a time to take it easy. At the *dojo* there is not a lot of time for dating; however there have been a few *uchideshi* who were very good at managing their busy schedules and who enjoyed a fairly active social life. And, as to be expected, there have been a few *uchideshi* that have dropped out of the program due to the rigorous conditions of training and *dojo* responsibilities.

There are, however, days when the *uchideshi* can enjoy themselves without reservation. *Bureiko* is one such time for letting loose—a party where the *uchideshi* can eat, drink, sing and dance to their heart's content. "All right, let's party tonight!" Following the call, the *uchideshi* rush out for supplies. Without wasting any time, preparation for the feast begins with great anticipation for the fun to come.

Young *uchideshi* are known to have healthy appetites, but their cooking skills don't always allow them to satisfy their cravings for delicious meals. The dishes prepared for the *bureiko* party are a welcome delight. What further serves to make a *bureiko* special is that the *uchideshi* don't have to take care of the *senpai* during the party. In fact, the *senpai* serve food and drink to the *uchideshi*. It is interesting for the *uchideshi* to see the *senpai* in a different light for the first time. And the *uchideshi* are amused to discover that the *senpai* who is usually the most severe can't drink more than two beers without falling asleep, or that the *senpai* who is usually the kindest gets cranky as the evening wears on. Learning about the personal traits of the *senpai* can be quite entertaining.

By the end of the first term, the *uchideshi* begin to see warm hearts in otherwise stern *senpai*. *Bureiko* provides a wonderful opportunity for students at all levels to stand on the same stage—all as students of Aikido. This leads to a better understanding of each other and the training they have been going through together.

離場

28 *Rijo*
(Leaving the *Dojo*)

EARLY IN THE morning on the day he is to leave the *dojo*, an *uchideshi* kneels quietly on the mat and bows to the front. After completing a three-month term it is time for him to make a fresh start back home.

Some continue on to their second term of *uchideshi* training by applying at the Nippon Kan office. For those who are leaving *uchideshi* life, a special ceremony is held in their honor during black belt class. Watching the ceremony are both the stern *senpai* and the *senpai* who had kindly taken the *uchideshi* under his wing. The *uchideshi* receives a certificate, and as a graduate member of the *dojo* staff, is welcome back at any time. He receives a round of applause and warm smiles from instructors and fellow students.

The *senpai* have no reason to dislike a new *uchideshi,* but especially in the beginning of their training, the new *uchideshi* are treated in a rather cold and strict manner. This is only because the *senpai* want the *uchideshi* to complete the program by themselves for themselves. It is actually very difficult for the *senpai* to be distant or stern with a new *uchideshi,* since, like everyone else, they are basically kind at heart and want to be accepted and liked by others. It is especially difficult for the *senpai* in the beginning months knowing that a new *uchideshi* arrives so full of hope and expectations. Not knowing their good intentions, there have been occasions when a newly-arrived *uchideshi* does not understand and is angered by the *senpai's* words and behavior. Patience and perseverance reveal the true intentions of the *senpai.*

The *uchideshi* who complete their training are not necessarily super athletes or super martial artists. They are just patient and persistent in their training, trying over and over again. They are able to shed their past and perform their tasks as directed. *Uchideshi* training is somewhat like trying to carry water in a bottomless bucket. After all, life is like continuously carrying water in a bottomless bucket into a bottomless canyon. Discovering the bottom of the canyon is not the goal of *uchideshi* training, neither is making a pond at the bottom. The action of carrying the water itself is the goal of this training.

After completing his term, this *uchideshi* returns to his home elsewhere. Mission accomplished! Good work! The living quarters that he used are left spotlessly clean. All things are in perfect order. The plants are lively, showing the care they have been given.

"I wonder," this *uchideshi* ponders as he takes one last look around the room, "Will the next *uchideshi* notice the plants?"

II

稽古編

Practice

年越稽古

1 *Toshikoshi Geiko*
(New Year's Eve Practice)

AT 11 O'CLOCK ON New Year's Eve, about the time when parties all over town are really getting rolling, students at Nippon Kan gather to begin the practice that will take them into the New Year. The *dojo* has already been thoroughly cleaned in anticipation of the events to come. Preparations for the New Year's ceremonies and festivities (*Shogatsu Shitaku*) begin each year on December 27th. Tonight's ceremonial practice is held to reflect the passing of the old year and to welcome the hope and promise of the New Year.

This traditional ceremony is Shinto in origin, and follows a very specific order of events. It begins with *Oharai* (the cleansing of evil spirits), followed by *Norito Sojo* (the formal reciting of Shinto prayer), and *Honoh Enbu* (an offering demonstration). *Honoh Geiko,* or offering practice, is then held, followed by *Misogi* (purification) and *Tamagushi Honoh* (the offering of evergreens). At midnight, *omiki* (an herbal rice wine) is ceremoniously poured for all attending and the arrival of the New Year is toasted. This special ritual leaves all who participate with a feeling of solemn appreciation.

This ceremonial practice began at Nippon Kan seven years ago. Before that time, the largest party of the year was held at the *dojo* on New Year's Eve. Booths were built, including a sushi bar that offered a vast array of specially-prepared foods. One year's records show that 1,800 pieces of sushi were made and consumed. At its peak over 350 people enjoyed the festivities, making it a very large party indeed. In its early days we felt that it was very important to expose the *dojo* to the community in as many ways as possible. Besides being a time to celebrate the New Year, this was also a good way to let friends, family and other members of the community stop by to visit the *dojo*. In 1986, we decided that it was time to resume the traditional activity of *Toshikoshi Geiko*.

There are some who miss the old days when lavish New Year's Eve parties were held, but there is another way of looking at it. A gathering of thirty-five or so serious Aikidoists can be just as important as 350 party guests. Although there is no longer a party held on New Year's Eve, there is a New Year's party on January 3rd, a yearly Nippon Kan tradition since 1987.

稽古始

2 *Keiko Hajime*
(First Practice of the Year)

A WARRIOR DRESSED IN traditional Japanese armor leads the ritual of *Shikofumi*—alternating left and right, the warrior raises his foot and stomps down on the mat, turning in all four directions. This is a part of the *Keiko Hajime* (First Practice of the Year) ceremony called *Musha Gatame*.

Although some participants may still be suffering from overindulgence at the New Year's party the night before, January 4th arrives and the First Practice of the Year begins at 6:00 P.M. and lasts for about two hours. The *dojo* is decorated with red and white striped banners, and the front altar is filled with gifts and donations from members and supporters. A bountiful array of fresh fruits, vegetables, seafood, *saké*, and dried foods are arranged on both sides of the *kagami mochi* (pounded rice cakes that are made specially as New Year's offerings) which have pride of place at the center of the altar. More students attend this special winter practice than any other event of the year. Even before the practice begins, the temperature inside the *dojo* has risen from all the excitement and activity.

Following a Shinto ceremony, a specially selected student or honored guest enters the *dojo* dressed in the traditional Japanese warrior's armor. It is his duty to perform the *Musha Gatame* ritual described above, to assure safety and prosperity for all involved in the *dojo*. After he has finished his performance, everyone stands up and shouts three times "*Ei, Ei, Oh!*" "*Ei, Ei, Oh*" "*Ei, Ei, Oh,*" following the lead of the warrior. This chorus is called *Kachidoki*. Traditionally, it is customary to break open a barrel of *saké* at this point, but in order to avoid spilling *saké* all over the practice mat, this last part of the traditional ceremony is not followed.

After the ceremony, speeches are given by senior students, many of whom have been with Nippon Kan since its beginning. A brief practice is then held, more as a formality than for actual exercise on this day. Following the practice, student ranking promotions are announced and certificates are awarded before the close of the evening's events.

初心者稽古

3 *Shoshinsha Geiko*
(Beginner's Practice)

WITHOUT FAIL, ON the first day of beginner's class our new students can be found doing a variety of interesting warm-up routines before class begins. Some practice Karate stances or Yoga poses they have learned elsewhere, while others sit meditating. Some just stand in the middle of the *dojo* looking slightly lost.

The beginner classes are considered the most important of all levels of classes offered at Nippon Kan. Every advanced student at the *dojo* has gone through these beginning levels. And without the continuous participation of new beginning students, the *dojo* would not continue to grow.

Beginner's classes start in January and are repeated every eight weeks, totaling six sessions a year. One session is six weeks long and meets twice a week. There is a two-week break between new sessions. There are four sections (or time slots) in one session, and it is not uncommon to have anywhere from eighty to 100 new students beginning each session. Unlike some other martial arts *dojos,* new students interested in practicing Aikido are asked to wait until the next beginner's class begins, instead of being allowing to join general practice immediately. In our experience, it is better for new students to join a class geared specifically toward a beginning level, where their needs might be better met.

On the first day of beginner's class, the office staff and instructors get nervous, too—not only just the new students!

黒帯稽古

4 *Kuro Obi Geiko*
(Black Belt Practice)

DURING THE BEGINNING and general classes, much time is spent going over the philosophical aspect of our Aikido practice. Especially in the beginning classes, the techniques taught are kept rather simple so that students can concentrate more on the "feeling" of the movements. The movement is more dance-like and there is not a lot of attention paid to precise detail.

During black belt class, however, movements and techniques that are too advanced for less experienced students are taught and practiced. When students reach the black belt level, they work on techniques that are more effective and strong. Black belt students spend more time analyzing and trying to improve their techniques, working to achieve better mastery of their movements. This class also focuses on how to teach newer students and how to avoid accidents during practice. The practice is often very regimented and challenging.

Black belt practice is held every Monday as the third class of the evening. In addition to concentrated practice, the black belt class also serves another purpose. It is a once-a-week opportunity for long-time students to get together and work on their "communication skills." Students who have continued their practice long enough to achieve the level of black belt have spent many years at the *dojo*. In some cases, these students are no longer in a position to be able to attend classes every day. With many outside responsibilities, they attend less frequently, and for them Monday night is a the time to spend with old friends. Officially, this is a time to enjoy a hard practice, a cold beer, and the company of old friends.

5 *Getsurei Geiko*
(Monthly Practice)

ON THE FIRST Wednesday of every month, the third class of the evening is designated as *Getsurei Geiko* (monthly practice). This class is reserved for students who are third-*kyu* (third-level brown belt) and higher in rank. At Nippon Kan, third-*kyu* level students wear a *hakama* (a pant-like overgarment worn over their uniform pants). At this level students become "*hakama* members."

Over the Nippon Kan office phone, a child can be heard crying and a voice shouts out over the ruckus, "Sorry, I can't come to monthly practice tonight. I have to babysit my kids." The office staff person responds genuinely, "Not a problem, we understand. Good luck!"

There are eighteen classes taught each week at Nippon Kan, and with the exception of a few special classes (like black belt class), any student who has completed the beginner course can participate in any classes they choose. For example, any student of third-*kyu* level or above can keep attending beginner-level classes as long as they fully understand that the practice is specifically geared for beginners and not for students capable of more complicated techniques. In fact, experienced students are encouraged to attend beginner-level classes to help new students learn more easily. Of course work schedules, family activities and other outside responsibilities often dictate which classes one may attend. If the *dojo* had strict rules on which classes students could attend, overall attendance would drop. Therefore, we keep an open-attendance policy as long as each student participates at the level of instruction the class has been designed for.

Due to busy schedules, students sometimes fall into specific patterns of days they are able to attend practice. When this happens there is no chance for them to get to know and practice with students who regularly attend other classes. For the development of students third-*kyu* and above, it is important to maintain regular communication with other students who are at similar levels. Communication promotes understanding and this is helpful in keeping the *dojo* running smoothly. Therefore, the third class of the first Wednesday of every month is designated as a special class for all "*hakama* members" to attend. At the beginning of class, important announcements are made and issues concerning the *dojo* are discussed. This is an important opportunity to take part in *dojo* operations.

If a student must be absent for one of these special classes, he or she is expected to call in to the office and excuse themselves prior to the beginning of class. An absence without an excuse can hurt a student's ranking standing, and repeated absences could result in the student's removal from candidacy for the next upcoming promotion.

Although our members may be strong practicing on the mat, it does not mean that they always get their way at home. That's OK . . . family comes first.

短期滞在稽古

6 *Tanki Taizai Geiko* (Short-Stay Practice)

TAKING OFF FOR Denver, a determined young man looks back at his girlfriend's sad face in the rear-view mirror. "I want to become a black belt Aikidoist. Please understand. Just bear with me until I get it."

Some students visit Denver on weekends to practice Aikido from towns too far away for a daily commute. For these students, we provide lodging facilities. Many surrounding towns are a two or three-hour drive to Denver—not an easy commute before and after practice. During the week classes are held in the evening, which makes it even harder for out-of-town students to participate in classes and then drive back home.

The weekend short-stay program offers two classes in the evening on Fridays, one class on Saturday morning, and another on Sunday morning. Students can spend Saturday afternoon sightseeing, shopping, visiting friends, or practicing in the *dojo* on their own. After class has finished on Sunday morning there is plenty of time for a leisurely drive back home. The *dojo's* lodging facility is always open for any Aikido student who wishes to make use of our weekend short-stay program.

Not only students who live in Colorado, but also those from Kansas, Wyoming, and other neighboring states take advantage of this program and practice Aikido at the *dojo*. Some students choose to spend a whole week or even two weeks at the *dojo*. Although the visits are relatively short, it can be a nice retreat to spend a few days away from normal routines. The *dojo* is for students; without students there would be no *dojo*. It is the *dojo's* obligation to provide as many opportunities for practice as possible for those who seek it. Of course, this program, like the others, depends on a clear sense of responsibility and mutual trust.

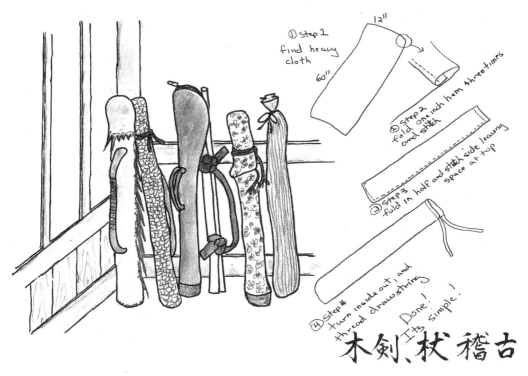

① Step 1
find heavy cloth

12"

60"

② Step 2
fold one inch hem three times and stitch

③ Step 3
fold in half and stitch side leaving space at top

④ Step 4
turn inside out, and thread drawstring

Done!
It's simple!

木剣、杖 稽古

7 *Bokken to Jo Geiko*
(Wooden Sword and Staff Practice)

AT NIPPON KAN, practicing with the *bokken* (wooden sword) and *jo* (wooden staff) is considered a basic fundamental in understanding the open-hand movements practiced in Aikido. Beginning-level students are taught how to move with these wooden weapons. Some Aikido *dojos* reserve their *bokken* and *jo* practice for advanced students only, but we feel that practicing with *bokken* and *jo* is a vital tool to be used from the beginning of everyone's training.

By practicing proper movement with the *bokken* and *jo* we can learn the roots of our Aikido techniques. We can learn proper movement of our bodies, balance, and timing. So, it makes sense to practice with the *bokken* and *jo* from the beginning of one's training.

Aikido originated from martial arts that were practiced by the *Samu-*

rai (warrior) class in Japan's early history. Naturally, *Samurai* carried swords at all times and used them, if necessary. When they chose not to use their swords (or happened to be caught without them), they used open-hand techniques that utilized much of the same movements used when they had swords in-hand. These techniques of unarmed combat were practiced as a part of a *Samurai's* training.

Later, during the Meiji Period, the government prohibited anyone from even carrying a sword. Martial arts training during this era became focused on hand-to-hand techniques. Shortly after World War II, during the Showa Period, the American military prohibited the practice of all martial arts that included rigorous or aggressive movements. In compliance at that time, Aikido—where it was allowed to continue to be practiced—suspended the use of weapons.

Today at Nippon Kan, practice with wooden weapons is incorporated in all classes. In addition, there are classes specifically geared to teaching wooden sword and staff movement and its relation to open-hand techniques. Many different weapons cases line the wall near the entrance to the *dojo*. One is made of Indian paisley, another neat and expertly crafted by a loved one at home. One set of weapons are fastened simply with a belt. Someone has even used a rifle case to bring his weapons to class! Each weapons case is unique and shows the imagination and creativity of its owner. I have always told my students that between expensive readymade weapons cases and handmade weapons cases, handmade cases are much more valuable. It is better not to be so particular about looks, and concentrate more on practice.

子供指導稽古

8 *Kodomo Shido Geiko*
(Teaching Children)

It's Saturday morning, just before children's practice begins. "OK, everybody listen up! Today is a special occasion. We have decided to take you all out for ice cream after class is over, so practice hard!" You can imagine how energetically the children practice this Saturday morning.

Children's Aikido classes have been taught at Nippon Kan ever since it opened over fifteen years ago. My 1993 book, *Children and the Martial Arts: An Aikido Point of View*, came directly from my experiences teaching this children's class. This book goes into much detail about how martial arts training can influence children's growth and development. There is no other class in which we can learn so much from teaching. For this reason, teaching the children's class is an excellent opportunity for instructors.

In many cases, the children who are sent to the *dojo* to take Aikido classes carry with them their parents high hopes and expectations. Whether or not the child continues the class may have something to do with the level of their parents' expectations. Interestingly enough, it seems that the children who have the highest expectations put upon them struggle the hardest to free themselves from their parents' expectations. High expectations can be a heavy burden to carry so the first thing we try to do is to relieve the children from the burdens they may be carrying. Children cannot move freely when they feel they are expected to perform. Instead, the instructors try to get in touch with the children's hearts and minds to bring out the natural innocence inside them. Once in a while, an instructor's money earmarked for pizza and beer that evening turns into ice cream cones after class for the kids instead.

遠征稽古

9 *Ensei Geiko*
(Practice Tour Away from Home)

For almost a decade the *dojo's* annual trip to the East Coast has been something to look forward to. After a class on the beach, off come sweaty *keiko-gis* and *hakamas*, revealing worn uniform pants and knees that haven't seen the sun all winter long. The corners of this "beach boy's" belt are worn white from years of practice and sweat. Everyone sucks in their stomachs, wishing they had done a bit more training before this trip to the beach.

Throughout the year there are seminar tours to other *dojos*. Some are nearby and some are several hours travel by plane. Practicing away from home is called *Ensei Geiko*. Students look forward to the annual trip to the Atlantic coast. In the fall, many students from the coast and other parts of the country come to Denver to take part in seminars held at our *dojo*. Nippon Kan is an independent *dojo,* allowing visits from friends from different groups and organizations who in turn invite Nippon Kan to participate in their seminars. This allows us to open our doors to all who wish to practice here, and many visitors do come each year.

Ensei Geiko is not only a chance to practice and share with students from other places. The hosting *dojo* always offers the highest level of gracious hospitality. It is important to enjoy practice, and having the opportunity to do some sightseeing and swimming on the beach makes it even more enjoyable. *Ensei Geiko* provides a chance for students to make new friends and catch up with old friends.

10 *De Geiko*
(Practicing at Different *Dojos*)

WHEN TRAVELING ON an airplane, a bag full of uniforms is not much of a problem, but a weapon case can be. To avoid unnecessary trouble, it might be a good idea to carry a set of fishing poles along with your *bokken* and *jo,* and avoid using the word "weapons!"—security officers unfamiliar with Aikido practice might get the wrong idea. I'm just joking of course, but it can be a little confusing at times.

When there is a seminar held at another *dojo,* instructors and assistant instructors are sometimes sent to participate. In these cases, most of the instructor's expenses, including air fare and lodging, are paid for by Nippon Kan. There are many Aikido seminars of different levels throughout the United States and it is sometimes difficult to determine to which ones we should send Nippon Kan representatives. In many cases, instructors are sent to seminars organized by *dojos* or instructors active in innovative methods and activities.

At the beginner level, Nippon Kan students are advised "For now, your *dojo* is here at Nippon Kan. We ask you to diligently practice here until you are comfortable calling this *dojo* your home." I feel it is important to form a foundation based on your home *dojo's* principles and style before venturing out to sample different approaches to Aikido practice. There are some students who travel frequently to attend seminars. Some proudly attest to how many different seminars they have been to and how many instructors they have met. In the beginning of a student's training, instead of trying to build a repertoire of different styles picked up from outside seminars, it might be better to concentrate on developing a basic foundation.

Once the basics have been sufficiently mastered and the primary philosophy behind activities at the *dojo* fully understood, students can then become more open to different styles of practicing Aikido. At this level they are able to take better advantage of different *dojos'* teaching methods and choose what is important for their individual technical and spiritual development. For this reason only students who have achieved the level of instructor and assistant instructor are sent officially to participate in outside seminars.

As a parting message to these student representatives, they are reminded to never behave discourteously to the host *dojo* or other students. They are to act with the utmost respect for the host *dojo's* style and philosophy, never voicing criticisms or comparisons. "Make yourself as blank as possible, so that you can absorb their teachings to the fullest."

侍者稽古

11

Jisha Geiko
(Accompanying Assistant
to the Chief Instructor)

"ARE YOU SURE you checked carefully into the background of this *dojo* before committing us to this visit?" "Yes, sir! At least I thought so, even the letterhead says it is the Peace *Dojo*. . . ." With the accompanying assistant coordinating my visit as chief instructor, this conversation may unfortunately take place if the assistant did not do his or her job properly. Obviously, this assistant did not check into this host *dojo* well enough, which has led to an uncomfortable situation.

I receive many requests every year to teach seminars or classes at other *dojos*. I have come to realize that in some cases it is better not to visit Aikido *dojos* that I am not familiar with. I follow this rule with the express intention of avoiding involvement in interpersonal politics or unknowingly causing problems. In the past I used to visit any *dojo* upon request, but I learned that this policy led to my sometimes finding myself in the middle of an uncomfortable situation. One *dojo* that had invited me to teach a seminar even received notices from their federation threatening to expel them for inviting a guest instructor not affiliated with their organization. Causing problems is not my intention; therefore my teaching schedule is focused on *dojos* I am familiar with and on my practice at Nippon Kan.

Because working with students of different martial arts allows me a good opportunity to learn, once in a while I visit *dojos* of other martial art styles. Before committing to such a visit, it is the accompanying assistant's job to thoroughly check the background of those offering the invitation. Often, it is difficult to discern the style and philosophy of a *dojo* just by its name. Once, after accepting an invitation by a *dojo* recommended by another instructor, I arrived to find a big surprise—I discovered that this *dojo* was teaching a form of street fighting. Not only was the training hall itself not suited for the practice of Aikido, but we were shocked to find that students were smoking something strange behind the *dojo* between classes!

The responsibilities of an accompanying assistant are not merely to take falls (*ukemi*) on the mat for the instructor during class. He or she must also prepare for every aspect of the visit, including informing the hosts of what is needed and expected. The assistant must make all necessary travel arrangements, including meals, luggage transfer, schedules, etc. "Oh no, *Sensei*—I forgot to bring your *hakama*." "It's all right ... I'll wear yours." Alas! What was supposed to be a flashy demonstration for the assistant turned out to be an embarrassing one appearing half-dressed in front of strangers.

師範招聘稽古

12 *Shihan Shohei Geiko*
(Inviting High-Ranking Instructors)

"I THOUGHT I might stop by and visit your *dojo* for two or three days at the end of the month." "That's wonderful news, *Shihan* (a term for high-ranking instructors), but that doesn't give us nearly enough time to prepare for such a special visit." "Oh, don't worry about that. I just want to come and see you. Special preparations are not necessary...." Well, it looks like we are going to have our special visitor after all!

On the front page of Nippon Kan's general information flyer, it states that any Aikido instructor visiting the Denver area is welcome to come to the *dojo* and teach a class any time, schedules permitting. These flyers have been distributed all over the United States and, as a matter of fact, there have been instructors who have dropped by to visit and teach a class. This invitation is not limited to American instructors. One evening, we had the opportunity to have an instructor from France teach a class. He conducted the class mostly in French, which added to the exotic atmosphere of the evening.

For special occasions, specific instructors are often invited to come to Denver to teach. Because Nippon Kan is an independent *dojo*, instructors are welcomed from many different organizations. On several occasions *Shihans* who were my former teachers have been invited.

Ordinarily, I spend much more of my time demonstrating how to do techniques, rather than having techniques demonstrated on me. However, when these special instructors come to visit, I prepare myself to perform as assistant. In order to be able to do vigorous rolls without appearing out of breath, I lengthen my regular exercise routine for a few weeks prior to the visit. Strengthening one's wrists to withstand certain joint stimulation techniques (such as *nikkyo* and *sankyo*) takes more than a few weeks of special practice, so I hope that the guest *Shihan* will not demonstrate such techniques too intensely!

指導稽古

13 Shido Geiko
(Learning by Teaching)

"DON'T BE NERVOUS. Just think of them as a row of pumpkins lined up in front of you." A *senpai* gives advice to a new assistant instructor before he begins teaching his very first class. "Funny, my body does not seem to be reacting properly like it usually does." "Stop worrying" coaches *senpai*, "that is a normal reaction before teaching for the first time . . . you'll be fine."

Sometime after achieving the rank of black belt, students are often asked to volunteer some of their time helping in the office or assisting as instructors. This is considered an important part of training. Of course, students are not expected to begin teaching immediately after being promoted to black belt. Myself and the senior staff watch closely for the right time to begin this part of a black belt's training. But when the time does come, not much warning is given. During warm-up exercises, a senior instructor may approach one of the advanced students and say, "Teach the next class, OK?" It isn't good to refuse. Without good reason, if the student were to decline, he or she would not be asked again for quite a long time; there may not even be a second chance.

Even though one may have practiced many years to reach the rank of black belt, a sudden notice to teach a class of twenty or thirty students is not an easy task. Standing in front of students and leading them through a class can make even an experienced black belt nervous. Often what were only a few moments earlier simple exercise routines suddenly become hard to remember. It is easy to make a mistake in the exercise sequences and forget which exercise is next or lose count. To watch from the sidelines, this can be rather humorous. "He is usually so calm, he doesn't get nervous about anything." Everyone who has been an instructor remembers teaching his or her first class.

Teaching is just as important a practice as working out. Having a chance to stand up as instructor offers a unique opportunity to see oneself and fellow students from a different perspective. With years of practice, this kind of experience helps develop skillful instructors.

Students are quite honest when it comes to which classes they prefer to attend. If a class taught by a certain instructor is not interesting, students don't come to their following class. New assistant instructors pay a lot of attention to class attendance, and get seriously worried if the numbers begin to drop. Learning how to deal with this type of situation is also a good lesson. Taking positive steps toward solving problems improves the quality of an instructor's personal growth. By going through each stage of the teaching process, new assistant instructors gradually bid farewell to pumpkins and a case of the butterflies.

他武道稽古

14 *Tabudo Geiko*
(Practicing Other Martial Arts)

WE OFTEN SEE beginning students warming up with exercise routines learned in other martial arts such as Karate and Taekwondo. The instructor will ask these beginning students firmly to stop for a very simple reason: this is an Aikido *dojo*, and we are here to practice Aikido. Some beginning Aikido students who have practiced other martial arts unfortunately tend to constantly compare what they are learning now with what they have previously learned from other martial arts. This can become a hindrance to learning Aikido smoothly. Students who demonstrate their experience with other martial arts tend to confuse other students, especially beginner, fifth-*kyu*, or fourth-*kyu* ranked students. If a new student does not refrain from demonstrating techniques learned in other martial arts after being asked to do so, he or she might be asked to leave the *dojo*.

However, special classes are held for students third-*kyu* and above where instructors from different martial art schools are invited to teach. For example, every year a six-week Karate clinic is held for advanced students at Nippon Kan. Third-*kyu* and above students have reached a sufficient level of understanding Aikido basics so that they are not confused by practicing other martial arts. For students at this level, an introduction to other martial arts provides a wider perspective from which to view their Aikido practice.

It is often said that Aikidoists don't know how to deal with hard punches and powerful kicks. In order to overcome this handicap, Joko Ninomiya *Shihan*, of Enshin Karate in Denver, is invited to teach. Ninomiya *Shihan* and his students are very open to the idea of exchanging ideas on practice. Enshin Karate utilizes circular movements not unlike those used in Aikido, and their power is astonishingly strong. The gracious attitude and manner of Ninomiya *Shihan*, who seems happy to give us instruction, are valuable lessons for Nippon Kan's advanced students.

15 *Kyui Betsu Koshu Kai*
(Seminar for Each Rank)

"Now THAT I have explained in detail, let me show you what the principles of the technique look like." Sitting in *seiza* for long periods of time can have interesting effects. For most students who are not used to doing so, the result is usually that their feet go to sleep. After listening to my lecture, an *uke* (assistant on whom techniques are demonstrated) stands to join the instructor for the demonstration. Unfortunately, his numb feet can't cooperate and he misses his target. We call this "*Sensei* Power."

After completing the six-week beginner's course, some students choose to join the *dojo* as regular members, at which time their class attendance is monitored daily as part of the criteria for ranking promotion evaluation. Promotion evaluation criteria also includes seminar attendance, participation in volunteer work projects, technical improvement, and attitude. At Nippon Kan there is no testing for ranking promotion evaluation.

Usually, testing for rank promotion is a very good source of income for *dojos*. Some *dojos* put a strong emphasis on testing, conducting tests several times a year. Charging fees for testing and promotion certificates is how some *dojos* survive financially. Nippon Kan tries to approach the subject of promotions from a different point of view. When testing is emphasized, students tend to focus only on what they need to learn to pass the next examination. This can inhibit a student from genuinely learning the art as a whole. Myself and the instructor staff work with the students on a daily basis, and we know how much each student has advanced by watching his or her progress carefully. With this approach, we see no need for testing. Deciding whether or not to promote a student based on a testing demonstration that lasts only a few minutes is a difficult thing to do.

Instead of testing, Nippon Kan holds a series of seminars according to rank, so that, generally, all the students attending are at the same level. In this way, the seminar can be focused on what is needed at that rank's level. By attending these seminars, students can concentrate on specific areas within their level of experience.

Every student is an individual, of different ages, learning abilities, and physical limitations. There are many aspects of which systematic testing cannot judge the progress of each student fairly. It is necessary to evaluate not only a student's level of skill, but also their attitude toward practicing Aikido and their understanding of the *dojo*. These are all very important factors when considering ranking promotion.

16 *Shunki Koshu Kai* (Spring Seminar)

THE LARGE GYM is crowded with students attending the *bokken* and *jo* seminar held in February each year. This is an important seminar for students of all levels. The effectiveness of open-hand techniques used in Aikido is directly related to the amount of practice done with the *bokken* and the *jo*. To help beginning students learn open-hand techniques more easily, special *kata* (patterns of movement) with the *bokken* and *jo* are taught. Students generally become familiar with these *kata* before they reach the rank of third-*kyu*. Nearly two decades ago, I created the eighteen-step *jo* pattern (*Jo no Kata*) that is now practiced in many *dojos* throughout the United States. Today there are several *katas* practiced at Nippon Kan that I created for this purpose.

One goal of the Spring Seminar is to raise funds to support Nippon Kan's public service projects throughout the year. Our practice is not only limited to working on techniques inside the *dojo*—practice extends beyond the mat and includes making positive contributions to our community. This is an important objective of Aikido training and part of the teachings of Morihei Ueshiba. Becoming "one in harmony with the universe" starts at home. Rolling up our sleeves and helping those around us is one way to make this philosophy more than just words.

夏期講習会

17 *Kaki Koshu Kai* (Summer Seminar)

THE *dojo* BECOMES a very busy place with preparations for the annual summer seminar held each Labor Day weekend. This four-day seminar is one of the largest events held at Nippon Kan. Following two days of practicing empty-hand techniques at the *dojo*, the highlight of the seminar is a day spent in traditional outdoor training in the Rocky Mountains to work on *bokken* and *jo* practice.

As with any other seminar, the Labor Day Seminar proceeds smoothly once it gets rolling. The hardest part for the student staff organizing the event is the planning itself.

Schedules for the seminar are announced earlier in the summer. Then, about a month before the seminar, it is time to get busy organizing home-stay arrangements for guests and recruiting volunteers for various duties and activities. Special attention is paid to organizing the caravan of cars that must transport participants and equipment to the mountains on the third day of practice—a two-hour drive to reach the mountain practice site. A set-up crew leaves a day earlier to prepare the site. On the day of mountain practice, about thirty vehicles (plus an emergency medical vehicle, refrigerated truck, and an equipment truck) leave the *dojo* early in the morning in a long procession headed for the mountains. There is an impressive amount of food and equipment to be transported. The lead car and the "sweep car" in the rear keep contact by radio, making sure that everyone arrives at the site together.

Once in the mountains, the set-up, cooking, first-aid, refreshment, and instruction crews demonstrate highly efficient teamwork working together to coordinate the day's events.

Practice consists of students working their way through obstacle courses and outdoor circuit training with *bokken* and *jos*. The day's practice ends dramatically with over 100 students joining in moving meditation in a natural amphitheater in the rocky cliffs. Students sway to music echoing down the valleys from several speakers. All those participating get caught up in the breathtaking beauty of nature surrounding them.

The purpose of the summer seminar is not just to work on learning new technical skills. More importantly, each student must learn to work with fellow students to bring this large scale event to a successful conclusion. This kind of training and experience is the most important part of participating in the Labor Day Seminar.

Returning to Denver with dusty faces, hoarse voices, and blistered hands, there is nothing like a frosty mug of beer. Only those who have been through a day of mountain training could know how delicious it tastes.

秋期講習会

18 *Shuki Koshu Kai*
(Fall Seminar)

THE FALL SEMINAR is held on Thanksgiving weekend. Fortunately, in the last few years the weather has not been too severe— one year the temperature never climbed above four degrees below zero. Regardless of the weather, part of this seminar's activities includes practicing outside. Students are told to gather their *bokkens* and line up outside, wearing sneakers. Even if it is literally freezing outside, everyone jogs in orderly lines to the nearby park, keeping up morale by cheering in unison. Footsteps echo in the cold air, and steamy breath forms frost on mustaches and eyebrows. Students look at one another's red cheeks and noses and laugh, only to find that the muscles in their faces are stiff from the cold.

Of course, emergency vehicles are standing by in case anyone becomes a little too cold. For students used to living with heat and air-conditioning, it is quite an experience to face what feels like succumbing to overexposure to the elements. After completing an hour of this challenge in the cold, the students jog back to the *dojo*. Those who had complained about the *dojo* being chilly before practice began suddenly marvel at how warm it now feels on their return.

By experiencing the cold, one can appreciate even the slightest amount of warmth, and by experiencing unbearably hot days, one can appreciate the coolness of evening. To better understand and appreciate life, we sometimes have to bid farewell to selfishness and comfort. With an attitude of appreciation, cold can be warm and hot can be cool. As the beginning of this fall seminar nears, the staff hopes it will snow.

Being able to physically withstand the cold is not what is important—what is important is to discover new awareness through this kind of experience. This is the real reason for jogging out into the cold. Otherwise, it would be merely an empty demonstration of "macho" prowess.

19 *Keiko Osame*
(Last Practice of the Year)

THE *dojo* HAS already been spotlessly cleaned in preparation for welcoming the New Year. The students rise and make a toast, "*Kampai!*" (Cheers!)

On December 28, the last practice of the year is held. Most traditional *dojos* throughout the world hold their last practice on this day. After practice, there will be no classes held until *Toshikoshi Geiko* on December 31. During the day of this last practice of the year, the *dojo* is thoroughly cleaned. This is called *Susuharai*.

Since the *dojo* is cleaned every day there is little actual need for an especially thorough cleaning. But *Susuharai* serves another traditional purpose: along with the dust, any bad *ke* (luck) left over from the past year is swept out of the *dojo*. Following *Keiko Osame*, it is time to start preparing for the New Year.

This is a very busy time for me. It is traditional to express my appreciation by visiting many people whose generosity and understanding have benefited the *dojo*. I also make it a point to stop by and visit other Japanese martial arts instructors in town. In Japan, December is called *Shiwasu*, which means "the month that instructors run." In other words, instructors used to giving orders have to stay on the run themselves to keep up with all of the necessary duties.

"*Kampai!*" *Saké* is generously consumed (of course it is a ritual gesture for this ceremonial occasion), and everybody seems content as another good year of practice draws to a close. Time is forgotten as everyone spends the rest of the evening deep in conversation with their fellow students.

III

年事活動編
Annual Events

正月祝

1 *Shogatsu Iwai*
(New Year's Celebration)

STUDENTS WHO HAVE been practicing at the *dojo* since its beginnings—along with new students, families, and friends—traditionally gather together to celebrate the New Year on January 3rd. This is the most extravagant of all the parties held at the *dojo*. Special dishes are prepared for a traditional Japanese-style celebration by the Nippon Kan staff. Students bring favorite dishes and drinks from home to share, making the party an international culinary delight. There is singing, conversation, and plenty to eat and drink—everyone partakes to their heart's content.

The first activity of the year is *Toshikoshi Geiko*, which is held during the midnight hour between the evening of the last day of the previous year and the first day of the New Year. While this is a solemn ceremony, the party on the 3rd is a celebration. On this day, both new and old students, some who have since moved away, return to the *dojo* to visit with old friends. Students who are busy with their families and careers and cannot regularly attend the *dojo* pay a visit on this special day with their children. The days seem to fly by faster each year. Right before our eyes, they disappear—but the children's faces show how each and every day has shaped them. It is always a surprise to see how much each child has grown over the past year, and it brings such happiness to hear their young voices shout, "Happy New Year!"

In traditional Japanese *dojos,* the New Year's ceremony was a religious occasion held in order to present gifts from the sea, mountains, rivers, and farms to certain Shinto martial arts gods *(Yamato Takeru No Mikoto)* who served to protect the *dojo* and those associated with it. It was customary to offer these gifts to the gods, and then share this same food in their honor. Even today, by sharing with fellow students, the celebration becomes a wish for the safety of the *dojo* and further development of the martial arts.

The following day the first practice of the year is held.

春期奉仕

2 *Shunki Hoshi*
(Spring Volunteer Work Day)

My birthday is in May, and year after year students have held a birthday party to help me celebrate at a nearby restaurant. Attendance grew every year until it reached well over a hundred guests.

One year, however, after giving it quite a bit of thought, I said to my students, "My birthday comes once a year, and even though I am honored and very grateful for this party, if I spend this day only eating and drinking, what is there to show for it afterwards?" That year I decided to celebrate my birthday a little differently.

I was honored that everyone still wanted to celebrate the event, so I came up with another idea instead. The weekend day nearest my birthday was designated as "Spring Volunteer Work Day." One reason for this community volunteer work day is to take advantage of the work that can be accomplished by students who have been made healthy and strong by practicing Aikido. This is something special we can give back to community.

The volunteer projects are supervised by the Denver Parks and Recreation Forestry Department. In 1991 *dojo* members worked on refurbishing and lengthening a mountain hiking trail for the visually impaired. The Stapleton Braille Trail, located twenty-five miles west of Denver, gives visually impaired hikers a chance to go on a mountain hike guided by a leading cable and signs in braille. On the day of the work project, over sixty students volunteered to take part in the project and headed for the mountains for some hot, sweaty work.

One student busily clearing underbrush wondered out loud, "Why are we cleaning up the scenery on a trail for people who can't see?" This simple question was an opportunity for serious reflection. It is necessary to emphasize that volunteering is not done with the expectation of something in return—it is work done to the best of one's ability from the bottom of one's heart. The *work* is the goal, not rewards and satisfaction.

The following spring, the project was completed by pulling miles of cable through support posts to create the guiding cable around the course.

In recent years on Spring Volunteer Work Day, Nippon Kan students have planted flowers and flower sod in a local community baseball stadium and helped to plant more than 100 twelve-foot seedling trees in a popular city park. Next year will bring another worthy project. Leaving daily chores behind, the physical work in the mountains and local parks is an excellent form of self-discipline and a good exercise in teamwork. It has become a very important activity for the *dojo*, in harmony with the supporting community.

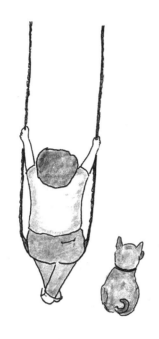

公共募金講習会

3 *Kokyobokin Koshu Kai* (Spring Fundraising Seminar)

ONE DAY, I was sitting at a table near the playground in Denver's Cheesman park, working on the manuscript for *Children and the Martial Arts: An Aikido Point of View* (published in April 1993.) It was a perfect place for writing about children, since many had gathered there that afternoon to play. There was one little boy sitting on a swing who seemed somewhat isolated from the other children. I began to talk with him. "What's that yellow ribbon you are wearing on your jacket? Do you know somebody who went to the Gulf War?" "Yes ... my daddy," replied the boy. This became my inspiration for the first public fundraising seminar in 1991. Aikido Nippon Kan's Weapons Seminar was held that February to raise funds for the children whose family members had been sent to war in "Operation Desert Storm."

In February 1992, another fundraising seminar was held to provide meals for the homeless at the Denver Rescue Mission. Since that time Nippon Kan has been preparing meals once a month at the mission. At each dinner, over 250 meals are served.

These spring fundraising seminars have become a yearly event, and a growing number of students have been participating in this activity, with over 150 students joining in this year's seminar. Nippon Kan also holds occasional "emergency" seminars to raise money for victims of hurricanes, floods, and other natural disasters.

People sometimes assume that Nippon Kan is a Japanese organization supported by Japanese business or government, and under this presumption there have been many requests asking the *dojo* for donations. In fact, I am the only Japanese national associated with Nippon Kan on a full-time basis; all other staff members are Americans. Regardless of the nationality of the organization, we all live in the same local community, and we feel it is our duty to work with the surrounding community wherever we can to help to improve it. Based on this belief, each year we choose a project to support and hold this special seminar to raise funds for the project.

Aikido is a martial art based on love and harmony. Preaching this without action is only reciting empty words. It is much more important to act.

国際留学生奨学制度

4 *Kokusai Ryugakusei Shyogaku Seido* (International Scholarships)

RECENTLY, TWO INTERNATIONAL students from Qatar joined the beginner's class. The office staff was not even quite sure where Qatar was located on the globe, much less knowing anything about the country. I decided to use this opportunity to increase the level of communication with people from different countries. The first step was to buy a world map and put it up in the office. To put my plan into action, I decided to waive all class fees for any international student studying full time at any college in the Denver area. By having international students practicing at the *dojo*, everyone receives a chance to improve their understanding of other cultures.

We have all made many discoveries. For example, devoted Muslim students will not bow to the front altar or to each other, as is regularly done in Aikido *dojos*. We have learned that this is not due to a lack of courtesy but is a reflection of their religious beliefs. As a compromise, Muslim students shake hands instead of bowing to thank their partners after practice.

The purpose of gathering people together from many different cultures to practice Aikido is not to deny anyone's cultural beliefs or insist that one manner of behavior is better than another. Often, we tend to follow the traditional customs we have been taught without allowing for a more expansive view of different customs and cultural traditions.

The *dojo* is a place for people to gather together and learn from one another. International students who have traveled from their home countries to study in the United States have given meaningful experiences to all *dojo* students. The value of their presence is many times that of any class fee.

出張演武

5 *Shuccho Enbu* (Public Demonstrations)

"NEXT TIME I am not taking an assistant who's so handsome!" I joked about all the attention my assistant received at a public Aikido demonstration.

During the late 70s, the martial arts gained wide popularity in the United States due to images created by Bruce Lee and other "macho" martial arts movie heroes. Trying to introduce Aikido among these stereotypical images was quite a challenge during the early years of the *dojo's* development. Giving demonstrations to promote the *dojo* was important to further its growth, but it was even more important to overcome the "movie star" image that had been created about the martial arts.

To accomplish this, I introduced classes and held demonstrations of other Japanese cultural arts along with those on Aikido. At that time, Nippon Kan held more than eight classes a day offering instruction in different aspects of Japanese culture. Demonstrations were given in over 80 percent of all the elementary, junior high, and high schools in the Denver metropolitan area. Because of this unique and authentic approach, the classes and demonstrations were a success, receiving frequent coverage from the news media.

Today, Aikido demonstrations are limited to those school programs that are seriously involved in learning about Aikido and Japanese culture. Although it may look like a cultural demonstration on the surface, performing at public fairs and festivals is just that—performing. Audiences who watch martial arts demonstrations while drinking beer and eating hot dogs are really there only to be entertained, and the purpose of a demonstration can get lost when it becomes only a sideshow attraction. Crosscultural exchange is a method of education, not just an opportunity to give a flashy performance of tricks and acrobatics in front of a cheering audience.

6 Noen
(Vegetable Garden)

"I CAN'T BELIEVE my eyes! These vegetables are beautiful!"

One of Nippon Kan's yearly activities allows students to learn about organic gardening. The garden was started as a creative solution to a problem—the lawn and the sidewalk on the side of the *dojo* was in need of repair. The cost estimates for replacing the grass and pavement turned out to be impractical, and the office staff, concerned about how to afford these costly repairs, came up with the idea of a garden. "Seeds are inexpensive and we can eat the vegetables!" This particular situation provided an opportunity for an interesting application of the Aikido technique of *tenkan* (turning 180 degrees to face the same direction as your partner).

Some who were skeptical about the project proclaimed, "It's impossible to make a vegetable garden here." But many students had extensive experience in gardening and offered us advice on how to carry out the project. To avoid the use of chemical substances, we used horse manure for fertilizer. The gardeners became the "Nippon Kan Farmers Club." As the club's enthusiasm outgrew the available garden space next to the *dojo,* club members negotiated an additional plot of land in a nearby community garden from the city, and a second organic garden began to grow. The vegetables produced are sold at a very low cost to students at the *dojo,* or used for specially-prepared *dojo* meals. All proceeds from the vegetables and dinners are used to help fund meals for the homeless at the Denver Rescue Mission.

Growing vegetables can take anywhere from one to three months. Sometimes, *uchideshi* or volunteers from Japan, Europe, or other parts of the United States who stay only a short time aren't able to watch the seeds they have planted come to harvest. Those who must miss the harvest are sent pictures by mail so they can share in the sense of accomplishment. Some students from large urban areas express sheer astonishment at what they helped to create: "Those little seeds grew to be such beautiful vegetables!"

歌声会

7 *Utagoe Kai*
(Singing Party)

IT HAS TO be in a garage. But the garage has to be a big one, one where we don't have to worry about disturbing the neighbors.

"Singing Parties" are held a few times a year. First, a suitable location must be found—preferably a garage or the like where we can eat, drink, and sing to our heart's content. Everyone is invited, including wives, husbands, kids, boyfriends, and girlfriends. The space is turned into a makeshift party room. Boards placed on barrels become tables. Paint drums and buckets turned upside-down make wonderful chairs. The party is divided into four groups that take turns singing songs. Since it is in a garage, it doesn't matter how loud the singing gets. Under these circumstances, normally quiet students sometimes turn out to be the loudest singers. Keeping the beat in time with the music, others begin dancing. This kind of activity develops camaraderie among *dojo* students. Activities like this also make it easier to identify the students who have true leadership ability.

Although Nippon Kan students have been known to have a healthy capacity for consuming liquid refreshment, there have been very few incidents of anyone losing control. While quenching their thirst, students also eat well, sing wholeheartedly, and dance with amazing energy. Of course, daily practice has a great and healthy influence as well.

It is not so good to sit and drink quietly. A party must be fun and entertaining, so students can explore different sides of themselves and learn more about their fellow students. The focus of the party is on having fun, dancing, and singing regardless of what beverages are being consumed—so everyone can join in. Once in a while, a few cars stay parked in front of the garage until the following morning. Safety is always a primary rule both on and off the mat.

勉強会

8 *Benkyo Kai*
(Study Sessions)

IT IS CUSTOMARY to have a Shinto altar in Japanese martial arts *dojos*. Nowadays, the altar is ordinarily located in the front of the practice area. Traditionally, there was an area slightly raised from the practice area where the director of the *dojo* sat to supervise practice, and a Shinto altar was built beyond that platform. Whether in the past or today, Shintoism is present at least symbolically in many traditional Japanese martial arts.

Occasionally, a Buddhist priest is invited to the *dojo* to recite from the *Okyo* (Buddhist scriptures) and give a talk about Buddhism. This is somewhat different from the norm in the West, where only one religion is usually represented at any specific location, if at all. In Japan, however, it is quite common for different religious customs and beliefs to manifest in the same place. In traditional Japanese homes, Shinto altars and Buddhist altars are found under the same roof. Some occasions are accompanied by Shinto rituals and ceremonies, and others by Buddhist rituals and ceremonies. In these same houses you may also find Christmas trees to celebrate that Western holiday.

In Japan, the basic philosophy of Shintoism is that all gods come from one. This belief allows one to explore and accept a number of religious teachings. A well-known Shinto teaching is: "Listen to as many teachings as are available, and learn the way to live."

At the *dojo,* study sessions are held each year to hear lectures by religious leaders and experts in various fields. Participation in these study sessions are open to all students, but are not mandatory. What one learns from these presentations is up to each individual. Sometimes after the lecture, senior students and guests from the community are invited to join the speaker for dinner.

Nippon Kan has a Shinto altar established in front of the practice area, but there are also many Buddhist influences present. Even the name "Nippon Kan" was given to me by Eido Shimada *Roshi* of the Zen Buddhist Temple in New York. Nippon Kan's logo of a child riding on the back of a cow also comes from a Zen Buddhist teaching story, depicted in the *Ju Gyu Zu* ("The Chart of Ten Cows") by the twelfth-century Chinese Zen master Kakuan Shion *Roshi.*

日本旅行

9 *Nihon Ryoko*
(Tours to Japan)

USUALLY TWICE A year, Nippon Kan plans tours to visit Japan. To date, there have been more than seventeen tours with over 200 people participating. These trips are not just sightseeing tours of popular areas such as Kyoto and Tokyo. Besides visiting famous historical attractions, the tours offer participants exposure to many cultural events, festivals, and experiences not available on more commercial excursions. In this way, the tours are more like a condensed crosscultural exchange program. In the Tohoku region of northern Japan there is a small village where part of this cultural exchange program takes place. During the visit, which may be from three to five days, there are many new experiences to be had: staying overnight in an ancient temple, enduring a fast, practicing *zazen,* (seated meditation), meditating under a water-fall, learning how to make local crafts, and even how to catch fish bare-handed.

On the tours, travelers bed down for the evening in local *minshuku* (Japanese tourist inns), family homes, *dojos,* and temples. These provide many opportunities to engage in more personal contact with local residents, creating friendships that bridge any barriers of language or custom.

For most tour participants this will be their first visit to Japan, and there are many things to learn. Like a flock of baby ducks, everyone stays close together while they get familiar with the lay of the land. The most amusing occurrences on the tours come from learning how to do the simplest of things—like taking a bath.

Even after being told, some have learned the hard way that soap is *not* to be used inside the bathtub, or that the plug in the tub should *not* be pulled out when you have finished your bath. These are both traditional bathing customs that most Americans are not familiar with, and much laughter ensues as friends watch their companions turn red as lobsters from the heat of the water, or an improperly tied *yukata* (informal cotton kimono) offers more of a view than intended. One tall visitor was caught innocently looking over the partition into the women's bathing area in a public bath—just because he was able to!

These downhome tours cover half the country. For many, they are the experience of a lifetime.

After returning from Japan

Living in Japan

米日相互体験

10 *Bei Nichi Sogotaiken*
(U.S./Japan Crosscultural Experience)

PEOPLE FROM ALL over the world come to visit Nippon Kan, but the majority of visitors are from Japan. In return Nippon Kan offers a program where students may stay in Japan for an extended period of time to study. In the mountains of Northern Japan lies the village of Naruse, where simple traditional lifestyles remain much as they have been for centuries. Naruse is the site of Nippon Kan's exchange program, which offers a unique opportunity to study authentic traditional culture on a firsthand basis.

Elements of Japanese culture and religion of which we are aware here in the United States, such as flower arrangement, tea ceremony, Zen, and the martial arts, all developed in a unique cultural and environmental background, and this background is inseparable from these forms themselves. It is important when looking at a flower arrangement or a *bonsai* tree to know and understand the background in which it was brought into being. It is the same with the practice of Aikido. If you wish to study and deeply understand Aikido's philosophy, it is important to know the "soil" from which it grew.

The purpose in our exchange program with Japan is to allow students today a chance to experience this historical background. The participants are able to experience events and lifestyles and to communicate one-on-one with villagers who maintain traditional ways of living. For this reason, students are not sent to large cosmopolitan cities like Tokyo or Osaka where much of this tradition has been lost.

The village of Naruse has a population of 3,600 people and a 600-year history. Students who go to live there are assigned to the village office. They are offered a wide variety of experiences, including volunteering in the village office, learning about farming, forestry, and animal husbandry, and of course practicing Aikido. Students learn much about the local culture and arts by living in the temple, with families as a home-stay guest, and eventually, if their stay is long enough, on their own.

Nippon Kan and the village jointly provide for all accommodations and $750 to $1,000 per month in scholarship assistance. In return, Nippon Kan hosts two to three members of the village each year. Our purpose is that these visitors become as well-informed about the United States as the students we send to the village become about Japan.

Because this program requires a special kind of student, candidates are selected only after they have been practicing at Nippon Kan for at least six months. In this way, they will have had sufficient background for the program to afford them a successful experience.

民具収集

11

Mingu Shushu
(Collecting Japanese Folk Art)

I BUILT THE Nippon Kan *dojo* as a replica of a traditional Japanese country house, and in earlier years its doors were opened to schools and other community groups for cultural demonstrations during the day while Aikido classes were not in session. Although the demonstrations were authentic and well executed, they lacked the physical evidence of the folk arts and craft history under discussion.

Before founding Nippon Kan, I worked as a folk art museum curator in northern Japan. On return trips to Japan, I began organizing my own private collection of Japanese folk crafts and tools. Over the past six years, and many trips later, the collection now on display at the *dojo* has grown tremendously. It includes tools and craft objects made and used by farmers, fishermen, and mountain men. Some of the items are over 200 years old.

When we think of Japanese arts and crafts, what usually comes to mind are swords, delicate porcelain objects, or woodblock prints. This is not a complete view of Japanese arts and crafts. This only represents the crafts of the elite and not those of the common farmer or fishermen whose skills and hard work were the foundation of Japanese culture.

Partly in reaction to World War II and Japan's devastating loss, a very elite and elegant portrayal of Japanese culture was conveyed to the West. It was a matter of self-esteem. However, at the same time, a cultural revolution was taking place in Japan as articles from the West became more sought-after than traditional Japanese items. Many ancient farm houses and artifacts were destroyed to make way for a new, more modern era. Even though these Japanese artifacts represented hundreds of years of history, many did not consider these treasures valuable because they did not represent refinement and modern ways. Currently, a new exhibition is being prepared along with accompanying photographs and descriptions of the folk arts and crafts that I have collected.

On my regular collecting trips to Japan, folk crafts and tools of all shapes and sizes are wrapped tightly and stuffed into huge bags. After being hand-carried, pushed, and dragged through trains, planes, and airports, U.S. Customs proves to be the most challenging hurdle. *"What's in the bag?" "A rice-straw crib." "Like for a baby?" "Yes, sir." "What is this?" "Oh, that is used to pound rice." "For what? How about this?"*

It proves to be a trying afternoon for everyone.

菜食会

12 *Saishoku Kai*
(Vegetarian Dinner Party)

"MIND IF I join you?" The cow from the Nippon Kan logo suddenly materializes at the dinner table. Well, it didn't quite happen like that, but there were enough vegetables harvested from the garden to feed a horse—or even a cow, as the case may be! Using the freshly-gathered vegetables, a vegetarian dinner party is created. For tonight's menu, seaweed, mushrooms, tofu, and *konnyaku* (yam cake) are added to the vegetables. Over a dozen dishes are prepared for the party. Sometimes a dish with a small amount of fish or chicken is added for variety. There are no set recipes for this occasion. Utilizing all available ingredients, I go to work. This is called *Yami Ryori* (cooking in a dark kitchen) because there are no set guidelines to follow. The recipe voted most popular this evening will be kept on record. Student guests at these vegetarian dinner parties are asked to make a small monetary donation that goes toward our Feed The Homeless project at the Denver Rescue Mission.

There are many important things to be learned from the garden project; for one, becoming more familiar with the soil and the gifts of nature. Also important is learning to share the harvest with fellow students and to give thanks by making a contribution to the community and helping to feed others in need.

遠来客接待

13

Enraikyaku Settai
(Entertaining Foreign Guests)

"IT IS DIFFICULT to imagine a view as spectacular as this," I enthusiastically explained from the passenger seat as the van approached the top of the pass. The vast Colorado Rocky Mountains spread in every direction. The driver, a student at the *dojo*, speaks up, "It seems that our guests must be tired—they have all fallen asleep. Shall we turn back?"

There are many guests who visit Nippon Kan from Japan. Most are not tourists, but instead come to Colorado to do field research, study, or work on special projects. After Nippon Kan receives a request from someone to visit Colorado, there are many arrangements to be made, depending on the visitor's focus. Usually, Colorado is only one stop on their agenda, and the visit may consist of only a few days. In rarer cases, visitors stay only one night in Denver. Overcome by a very busy schedule, jetlag, and the high altitude, many visitors have fallen asleep on route through the high Colorado Rockies. The *dojo* host staff responsible for these guests are fully aware of a visitor's condition, and make every possible attempt to ensure a satisfying and pleasant stay in Colorado.

With over 7,000 past and present students on file, Nippon Kan has vast resources for meeting visitor's needs. The *dojo* has worked with a number of Japan's major television networks, coordinating on-location filming sites, interviews, and logistics. To date, the *dojo* has taken part in over twenty television programs that were aired nationally in Japan. Based on Nippon Kan's principle of the importance of cultural exchange, we are very supportive of this kind of activity. This type of hospitality is always reciprocated when Nippon Kan students visit Japan.

秋期奉仕

14 *Shuki Hoshi*
(Fall Volunteer Work Day)

"*Sensei*, DO YOU think they'll deliver pizza to the middle of the park? We are going to need a lot of them," a student asks. Soon after, a young man with a puzzled look on his face approaches the group as they work and asks, "Are you the guys that ordered the pizza?" "Yes we are, what took you so long?" With that, the delivery boy lets out a sigh of relief and everyone laughs.

The Fall Volunteer Work Day takes place sometime before the Thanksgiving holiday. It is important for the students of the *dojo* to extend their practice of Aikido outside the confines of the mat. Sometimes a *dojo* can become closed to the rest of the world, often without realizing it. When this happens—even if everyone within the group

sketch

is content—the group can become isolated. This can be unhealthy and lead to stagnation.

Volunteer work is designed to encourage students to be proud and responsible members of the community by actively taking part in projects outside the *dojo*. It doesn't really matter what type of activity is chosen. As a collective body, the *dojo* offers its volunteer services to the Denver Parks and Recreation Forestry Department.

In the park where many students play or sunbathe during the hot summer months, students join forces to turn the flower beds, preparing them for next season's planting. This is simple, hearty manual labor. The soil becomes the mat and under a beautiful fall sky we prepare to practice. It is important that we shed any notion of making a contribution. This is time to work out, not pat ourselves on the back.

Fifteen years ago, before there was a *dojo*, a handful of students and I practiced *bokken* and *jo* in a corner of this park. Some of those students went on to become staff members of Nippon Kan. Today, it is amazing to see so many students working together in the same park, this time as volunteers. It would have been hard to predict so many years ago.

This project was adopted by the Denver Parks and Recreation "Hands on Denver" Volunteer program, and has since become a citywide project. Many other organizations and volunteers now help prepare the flower beds in parks all over Denver.

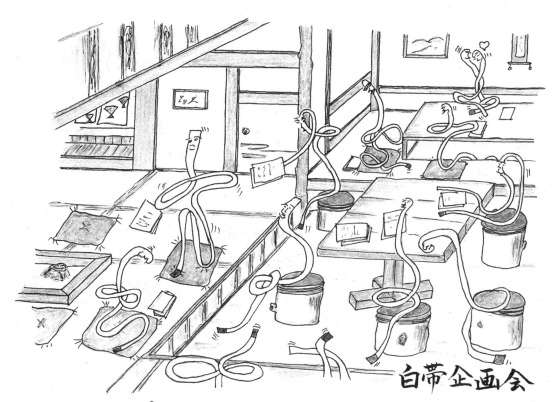

白帯企画会

15 *Shiro Obi Kikaku Kai*
(White Belt Project Planning)

OVER 500 NEW students enroll in the beginner's Aikido classes each year, and due to such a large number, it is impossible to remember the name of each new student. While many students take the six-week beginner's class, most do not continue their training after completing the course.

The students who do decide to continue their training become new regular members. In many cases, the first thing they do is buy a practice uniform, with a brand new *shiro obi* (white belt). Soon they begin to look as comfortable in their new uniforms as older students. The first major responsibility given the new students is to plan a Halloween Party for the *dojo*. Third-*kyu* (brown belt) level and above students stay out of this project planning, leaving it to the white belt students. The new students hold many project meetings, busily making all the arrangements that will turn the *dojo* into a haunted house. Posters and decorations are made, food is prepared, skits are rehearsed, and usually some kind of "chamber of horrors" is built.

It is sometimes difficult to discover all the characteristics of each new student just beginning their practice on the mat. While the white belt students are busy planning, the office staff pays close attention to discover among them potential future student leaders. This kind of project planning also offers useful training since it focuses on working together towards a common goal. It is an opportunity to begin to learn how to manage large-scale events—skills that will be needed for future projects. Such off-the-mat activities challenge students and open new avenues of interacting and working together.

Having gone through many experiences like this, new white belt students gradually become capable of handling many different responsibilities. It takes a long time and many projects before the brand-new white belt turns into a black belt.

年末衣類、硬貨寄付

16

Nenmatsu Irui Koka Kifu
(End-of-the-Year Clothing and Penny Drive)

THE *dojo* MAT is covered with clean, used clothing donated by students, and buckets full of coins are dumped in the middle of the mat for sorting. Every November, the *dojo* begins our annual End-of-the-Year Clothing and Penny Drive. The campaign is not for the benefit of the *dojo;* rather the clothes and money are donated to our Homeless Service Project. Students throw their spare coins into the large glass jar placed in the lobby. Some students collect coins all year and bring their small jars to the *dojo* during this initiative. Of course, the jar in the lobby is there throughout the year, but during November, as the drive reaches its peak, the coins fly in faster than ever. During this time, students are also asked to go through their closets and bring in any warm winter clothing that they no longer need. Each year, about 500 articles of clothing for men, women, and children are donated along with a five-gallon bucket full of coins and bills.

Senior students go through all the collected clothing, separate according to size, and put them in boxes. Coins are counted and deposited in the fund for Meal Service for the Homeless. There has always been a lot of support for this campaign. Everyone seems to enjoy joining in an effort that directly reaches so many people in need.

17 *Shokuji Hoshi*
(Meal Service for the Homeless)

HOMELESS PEOPLE START lining up outside hours before it is time for dinner to be served at 8:30 P.M. It's cold outside, but there is often no other way of getting a day's meal for those living on the streets. Some wait from early in the morning because they have no place else to go. The Denver Rescue Mission provides meals for its forty to fifty residents at 5:30 P.M.; then, at 8:30 P.M., 200 to 250 of the homeless who have been waiting outside are let in for a hot meal.

Under my direction, Nippon Kan provides a dinner at the mission once a month throughout the year, but a special dinner is planned for the middle of December. The funds raised through the garden project, fundraising seminars, and "penny drive" are used to put on this special dinner sometime between Thanksgiving and Christmas. Our goal is to serve over 250 eight-dish dinners. Preparations begin a few days in advance, and on the day of the dinner volunteers move into the kitchen of the Denver Rescue Mission in the early afternoon. Cooking so many dishes for such a large crowd is quite a different challenge than cooking one dish, or cooking for one person. Often, some of the students with less experience in the kitchen become overwhelmed by it all. These less-experienced chefs, mostly bachelors, nonetheless make a valuable contribution to the dishwashing team.

Since it is the Christmas season, a choir from a nearby church stops by the mission to sing a few Christmas carols. If the wishes and intentions of all those sitting and listening to the carols had come to be, there would not be any homeless people here this night. Everyone would have a home to go to, surrounded by their own loved ones singing carols. For countless reasons, conditions are otherwise this December evening. Many gather in the mission basement to hear the choir sing. When the choir finishes, the homeless people and the Nippon Kan staff applaud together, and share for a moment the same feelings. To the volunteers, it is a sobering Christmas celebration as each realizes that anyone of them could be there waiting for Christmas dinner next year. Later that evening, well past eleven o'clock, the volunteers leave the rescue mission. Back home in their own beds, they reflect that they have much to be thankful for.

正月支度

18 *Shogatsu Shitaku* (Preparing for the Coming New Year)

FOLLOWING *Keiko Osame* (Last Practice of the Year) on December 28, the *dojo* staff gets busy preparing for the coming new year. The thorough cleaning of the *dojo*, called *Susuharai*, has to be finished and *shimenawa* (special rice-straw rope decorations) must be placed at the front entrance and on the *dojo* altar. *Sakaki* (symbolic offerings which also decorate the altar) have to be prepared as well. Arranged flowers are placed carefully throughout the *dojo*. All of these preparations must be completed by noon on December 31st.

An essential part of any New Year's celebration is the making of *mochi* (pounded rice cakes). On the 28th or the 30th of December, *kagamimochi* (rounded *mochi* cakes stacked concentrically on top of each other) are placed on the altar and at other notable places in the *dojo*.

Mochi is made of sweet, sticky rice. After the rice is steamed, it is pounded in a giant mortar made from a hollowed-out tree stump until there is no trace of grain left. This requires quite a bit of physical strength and endurance. As the person pounding lifts the large wooden mallet, his partner uses his wet hands to flip the rice very quickly so that it won't stick to the mortar. Obviously, timing is very important! Sometimes, the rice is pounded by two or three people pounding in succession while another flips the rice with his hands. It may not seem too difficult to those looking on, but when others try it, they soon realize how much timing and endurance are necessary. The *kagamimochi* is placed on the front altar from December 31 until January 7, cracking as it dries. Traditionally, the cracks in the *kagamimochi* have been used to forecast what the New Year will bring.

After all the preparations have been completed and the *dojo* is filled with an indescribable air of sacredness, everyone anxiously awaits *Toshikoshi Geiko* (New Year's Eve Practice).

IV

運営編

Dojo Operations

受付

1 *Uketsuke*
(Reception)

THE DOOR TO the *dojo* opens and a man as big as Brutus from the Popeye cartoon steps up to the reception window. "Can we help you?" inquires the office volunteer on duty. "I want to learn self-defense," he says, looming in the doorway. The office staff look at each other quizzically, wondering what such a person might need self-defense against! Some new students leave the office staff speechless when they first enter the *dojo*.

The office reception staff has a very important responsibility: they are the first contact that a potential new student makes when he or she calls or visits the *dojo*. Frequently, the *dojo* receives calls from people who sound like they have just come from a martial arts movie. Visions of superheroes dance in their heads. When dealing with callers like these, experienced office staff keep their answers short and to the point. When a caller is excited, there is no use trying to explain what Aikido is all about. After the caller's excitement wears off, he usually tends to forget that he even thought about joining a martial arts *dojo,* and in most cases never comes in for training. There is not much point spending a lot of time on this kind of inquiry.

Dealing with people who come to the *dojo* in person to ask about Aikido training is another important task of the office reception staff. All potential new students are courteously given our general information flyer to take home, and they are allowed to observe an ongoing class for a few minutes. The general information flyer includes the dates of the upcoming beginner's classes, and the visitor is invited to return when the next session begins if they are interested.

In some cases, potential new students want to begin training that very same day, but the reception staff encourages them to wait for the start of the next beginning series. If they say they can't wait, we provide them with names of other Aikido *dojos* they might want to try. At Nippon Kan, it is our view that martial arts training must be considered a long-term commitment, and it has been our experience that someone who cannot wait for two or three weeks until the next beginner's session starts usually does not continue training for very long either. We won't enroll a student prematurely just to collect a class fee.

Our office reception staff has become quite skilled in being able to discern what potential new students are really seeking. It comes with experience—7,000 new beginning students have passed through Nippon Kan's doors at the time of this writing.

庶務

2 *Shomu* (Administrative Duties)

EVEN THOUGH MEMBERS of the office staff all wear the same uniforms at the *dojo*, they are all professionals in various fields. Perhaps it is due to their positions in the community that they perform their duties at Nippon Kan with such competence. There are hundreds of students from all backgrounds who practice at the *dojo*, and this increases the odds for unexpected events taking place. Faced with this constant possibility, it is truly a relief to know that our office staff can be counted on to deal with any situation.

Many tasks must be managed to keep the *dojo* running smoothly. The days when all that was required to manage a martial arts *dojo* were trophies to display in the window, a desk, and a phone, are long gone

... along with Bruce Lee. Fortunately for the last few years, the Nippon Kan office has been completely computerized.

Class attendance, membership dues, and daily accounting records are all tracked by computer. At the end of each month, attendance records and monthly balance sheets can be printed and analyzed. It is easy to go back a month or several years to compare figures by entering a few simple commands on the keyboard. Several of our students, professional computer programmers in high demand, developed these specialized programs. We can rest assured that they are sufficient for our needs. All Nippon Kan activities are organized and recorded by such capable office staff members. Healthy management and the steady operation of a *dojo* is the highest responsibility we have to our students.

3 *Kaikei*
(Accounting)

IT IS NOT unusual to hear the chief office staff accountant complain somewhat loudly, "We have got to cut back on spending! Don't you know what it is doing to us financially? There will be no more checks written this month, period ... end of discussion." To emphasize his point, he draws a picture of a skull and crossbones and tapes it to the *dojo* checkbook. This ultimatum is issued every month. In fact, it has become somewhat of an end-of-the-month ritual.

The *dojo* is maintained financially by student monthly membership fees. Over the last fifteen years, monthly fees have remained at thirty dollars, despite the dramatic increases in the cost-of-living index. What has increased in fifteen years is the number of classes and activities offered at Nippon Kan. This growth can be attributed to solid management. About five years ago, the subject of raising dues to forty dollars a month was presented for discussion. It was determined that the primary goal of raising dues was to finance activities at Nippon Kan. If this was already being accomplished, then current dues were sufficient since Nippon Kan's budget does not include brand new cars and trips to the Bahamas for instructors, as in the case of some high-profile profit-oriented martial arts *dojos*. At Nippon Kan, there has never been the intention to get rich by teaching Aikido, and the price increase was rejected.

Of course, we owe a great deal to the fine work of the office staff accountants who keep a close eye on the *dojo's* financial balance. A couple of days a week after classes, the chief accountants work on the *dojo* ledgers. Having brought us this far with limited funds, our accounting staff are truly heroes. In spite of a tight budget, our chief accountants always manage to reserve a small amount of funds for "wrap-up parties" after major Nippon Kan events. Everyone looks forward to these celebrations, and we have our dedicated accounting staff to thank for them.

4 *Kansa*
(Auditor)

A DANGEROUS WEAKNESS in any nonprofit organization can be a lack of accountability. While volunteers usually have a very positive attitude, they may not always see their tasks and duties through to completion. Unless a volunteer makes a grave mistake leading to serious consequences, their work performance is not likely to be questioned. This is entirely different in other businesses, where a clear chain-of-command and job performance evaluations are strictly maintained to keep operations under control. This is not as easily accomplished when the staff are unpaid volunteers.

Nippon Kan staff members are all volunteers. Because Nippon Kan teaches a traditional Japanese martial art, its system of hierarchy is also traditional. This structure makes the organization somewhat more manageable than other nonprofit organizations operated by volunteers.

We have had the experience of having a new office staff member come up with an enthusiastic new idea, only to be abandoned before the project was completed. One such volunteer proposed and took charge of an activity, then later declared that he had found a new interest and wouldn't be able to spend much time working on the project any more. You can imagine the loss in time, resources, and a sense of trust among students brought about by this lack of responsibility. For this reason, choosing volunteers for office staff is a very serious and very difficult undertaking. It is important to look for individuals who will complete the work they have begun.

Responsibility is also important in managing office supplies and inventory. The *kansa-yaku* (inventory control officer) inspects the office, counting pens, staples, paper supplies, and the like, making sure they are not being wasted. Often, other office volunteers hear him lecture on the importance of managing limited resources. After seminars, detailed reports must be filed by team leaders listing all supplies purchased, used, and left over. These reports are vital for analyzing projects and providing a resource of information for the future. Unless all team procedures and details are accounted for in the reports, they are not acceptable to the inventory control officer.

The role of an inventory control officer is crucial when managing an organization run by volunteers. If a loss or discrepancy is found, these two office volunteers might end up doing a lot of extra pushups and leg lifts during practice!

企 画

5 *Kikaku*
(Project Planning)

"Ponk needs what? What do you mean the doctor wants to give him a shot? Oh, it's only a routine vaccination ... We'll be there in the morning." This strange phone call is answered by the Nippon Kan chief project planner. Planning projects—from a major seminar to taking our reluctant *dojo* puppy, Ponk, to the vet—are all part of the planner's responsibilities. "I need more time, there aren't enough hours in the day." is a commonly used expression of the chief project planner. The many unique opportunities that this *dojo* has to offer its students is due in large part to the skill and dedication of the project planner.

All activities at Nippon Kan begin with the project planning staff. Since one of our *dojo* mottos is "Beyond the Mat," many of these projects involve students in projects within the surrounding community. Some projects are planned a year or more in advance, while others come up spontaneously and are organized quickly.

Project planning is important to keep *dojo* activities challenging and interesting. The planning teams use different approaches to keep students from falling into a boring routine. This staff, like all the volunteers at the *dojo,* also have busy careers and family responsibilities and do the work of planning *dojo* projects in their spare time. Trying to keep up with Nippon Kan's busy schedule can be a more difficult training than actually practicing on the mat.

If a stream stops running it becomes stagnant or may disappear altogether. But if the stream continues to flow, its waters remain fresh and clear. The success of *dojo* projects is not necessarily the first priority. More important are the lessons learned from working together as projects develop and unfold. This is an important secret to keeping a *dojo* healthy and alive.

6 *Seisaku*
(Production)

I SPEND COUNTLESS hours working on book manuscripts and other projects in my private office. Staff members stop by from time to time to "hang out" in my office — if they can find an uncluttered place to sit down. Since the nature of my work is very detailed, it is important that I maintain a certain order in my working environment. Socks left in the middle of the room must remain where they are, and last week's fish bones make very nice table decorations — otherwise, the feel of the room is not quite right for working! (Just joking, of course.)

Nippon Kan is quite active in publishing works that focus on the principles of Aikido as they are practiced at the *dojo*. It is important for me to continually strive to further understand American culture and the role that Aikido has to play in it. Equally important is to continually put ideas into practice and to learn and grow from the experience. The founder of Aikido, Morihei Ueshiba, often stressed in his teaching that changes and improvement must be daily events. Using his teaching as inspiration, we publish our discoveries and experiences so that others can join us and offer their own comments or criticisms. By making Nippon Kan's discoveries open to others, it helps us break away from ordinary routines and keeps us challenged with new ideas and input.

When I first began writing, I was very interested in reaching beginning students; therefore, my first book took the form of a primer. Today I am still interested in reaching beginning students, but with the books I am working on now, my scope has widened to include those in all stages of their Aikido journey. Once begun, it may take only a month or two to complete the original first draft. This is only the beginning of the process, however, since the manuscript needs to be translated into English, entered into the computer, and edited before it even reaches the layout and printing stage. This process takes many months— sometimes even years. It could not be done without the help of many talented staff members, and I thank them all wholeheartedly.

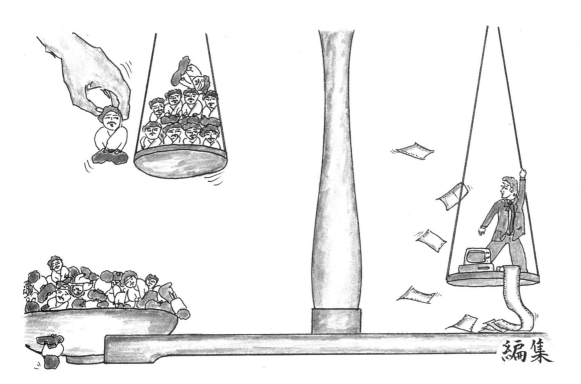

7 Henshu
(Editing)

IF NIPPON KAN's chief editor and I were to compare body weight, I would be the heavier. However my educational background and language skills are not nearly as weighty as those of our chief editor.

As I sit reading the newspaper in the inner *dojo* office, I can't help but overhear a strange, unintelligible conversation going on in the outer office, and I wonder what foreign language the people are speaking. I discover it is not people from a foreign country, but just our editing staff having a meeting. The language is far too technical for me to understand.

Once my original book manuscript has been translated into English, it is turned over to the editing staff. It is quite a challenge for them to keep the original content intact while making the language more compatible with English-speaking readers. If the editing staff were not personally familiar with my teachings and mannerisms, this would be an impossible task.

My level of computer knowledge is quite limited—my manuscripts are still hand-written and stored in three-ring binders. I am constantly amazed that the computer can locate any paragraph on any page in a fraction of a second—as simple as that function is for the computer. I have been learning, though, how to mimic the sound the printer makes when it begins to print: "z–z–z–z–z," and the sound it makes when it has finished printing, "*peroring–peroring–peroring.*"

The editors make their computers perform with such ease that they seem like magicians. The editing staff, mostly volunteers, are very talented with computers. Skill is important, but without their good hearts, my books would not exist.

8 *Shogai* (Outside Relations)

"EXCUSE ME, SIR. Just a moment … please don't misunderstand … we are an organization that teaches Japanese culture and a Japanese martial art, but we are not a Japanese organization." Sometimes this point needs to be clarified when working with vendors and other outside organizations. The name "Nippon Kan" causes many people to assume that Nippon Kan is a Japanese organization supported by wealthy Japanese foundations. The truth is, Nippon Kan is not a Japanese organization and has never received funds or been supported by the Japanese government, corporations, or other groups.

Because of the variety of activities Nippon Kan engages in, the ability to deal with organizations and groups not involved in the martial arts is a very important part of *dojo* project management. Arranging for space to hold events, for example, or renting the necessary equipment for an activity or project are all part of the thorough preparations necessary for successful programs. The manner in which we relate to others around us is vital to the health and success of the *dojo*.

As I have mentioned, in Nippon Kan's early days (it was then called the "Japan House Culture Center") we spent a great deal of time introducing Aikido and Japanese culture to local community groups and schools. We visited nearly all of the schools in the Denver metro area, giving demonstrations on various aspects of Japanese culture, art, history, and much about modern-day Japan. Through these experiences, I made a discovery that changed my attitude towards approaching the outside community and developing crosscultural understanding.

About six years ago I decided to discontinue most outside Aikido and cultural demonstrations. I began to realize that demonstrations of *sado* (tea ceremony) or *kado* (flower arrangement) for American audiences were serving to illustrate the differences rather than the similarities between the two cultures. It was like placing Japanese culture on one side of a wide river and American culture on the other, obscuring true human communication behind a mask of ceremony. I decided to focus for the time being on submerging myself in American culture, offering my Japanese flavor to Nippon Kan projects and activities. In this way, both cultures have a chance to stand for a while on the same side of the river. Having American and Japanese people working on a project together is a unique approach towards building awareness of each other's culture.

Whatever the project, the staff in charge of making outside arrangements has a demanding and important job. Not only does the job require diplomacy, but there is always the *dojo* accountant to answer to if expenses run too high.

9 *Koukoku*
(Publicity and Advertising)

IN 1979, WHEN the *dojo* was still in its infancy, one of our daily activities was to pass out flyers in town. Our objective was to let as many people as possible know about the *dojo's* activities. Discarded flyers were picked up, refolded, and passed out again.

Then and now, an essential aspect of successful *dojo* operations is advertising. There are many ways we advertise, including newspaper and magazine ads and direct mailings. For all printed materials, ad copy is written by the project planning staff and given to the graphic design department to be transformed into camera-ready art. At Nippon Kan, we regularly print general information flyers and newsletters. In addition, flyers are produced for special events. Mailings may be as large as 6,000 copies of a single newsletter or flyer. After the materials are printed, students are asked to volunteer a few minutes of their time after class to help fold, label, and sort them by zip code. By now, this activity has become a *dojo* tradition—students who are used to it have become quite efficient and can finish very quickly. All students can participate in such a project, and this helps encourage newer students to contribute to *dojo* operations. As a matter of course, students who actively volunteer for these kinds of activities are likely to become part of future management staff.

The *dojo* is not run by staff that provides services to paying students as if they were customers. All students participate in the making of their *dojo*.

撮影

10 *Satsuei* (Filming)

"THE PROBLEM IS not your hair, it's your face!" "The value of this video depends on its actors ... now get serious." "The next scene is the last one, isn't it?" Playful voices fill the *dojo* in between takes. "Five, four, three, two, one, action!" "What? Was it my turn? Oh, no!" Everyone laughs and teases playfully.

One of Nippon Kan's activities is video production. We have been involved in the production of over twenty-five videos, some produced independently and others in cooperation with major Japanese television networks. Several of the independently-produced videos are on file at the Denver community broadcast station's library and are run frequently for public viewing. The videos are not limited to teaching Aikido; there are also videos on Japanese cooking, travel in Japan, and others.

Watching a finished one-hour video, it is hard to comprehend the countless hours of time and energy that go into its production. After the original script is written, production proceeds step-by-step. First there are rehearsals, followed by the actual filming and editing process. Finally, the narration and soundtracks are added to complete the project. This process can sometimes take up to six months to complete.

Nippon Kan students make up the video production crews, although we do ask professionals to lend a hand and supply equipment. It is important to keep the production in-house so that the students have a chance to face the challenge and learn new skills from it.

The filming schedule calls for long hours and everyone involved works together from early morning until late at night. While the hours pass, another crew prepares lunch and then dinner for everyone. The tedious task of editing is done at night, after work, or on weekends. The crew spends countless hours of their spare time—sometimes up to fifteen hours a day—to get the project finished.

Producing videos may sound like a glamorous job, but in actuality it demands a lot of hard work. Teamwork, as always, is an important part of the script.

11 *Zatsumu*
(Handyman)

IN ANY *dojo* you visit, you will find at least one student staff member who is capable of performing all sorts of tasks and duties. This person is often quite unassuming, but once a tool is in their hands, they are transformed into a "superperson" able to get the job done quite efficiently.

In Japanese, there is the expression, *"En no shita no chikaramochi"* ("Strong men who support the foundation of a house"). At Nippon Kan, we are lucky to have brilliant computer programmers and equipment for them to use, but if a fuse is blown the work of this capable staff grinds to a halt. When a toilet gets plugged, it interferes with regular practice. Since we have many students from a wide variety of professions, repair work is usually taken care of in short order.

In addition to these "experts-in-their-fields," however, there is at least one student who is capable of solving all sorts of problems by himself. Thanks to the time and efforts of such talented individuals, most students do not experience even minor inconveniences at the *dojo*. Unfortunately, most students at the *dojo* are not aware of the work done by these handy helpers. Even more, those who form this foundation would rather not be singled out for what they contribute.

As maintenance work is required in any home or office, it is also important in *dojo* operations. All lighting inside and out must be kept in working order; leaky faucets are replaced; toilets fixed; house plants cared for so they stay green and lively; the *dojo* is kept warm, etc. Often these things go unnoticed or are taken for granted in our daily lives. If you stop and look around, you will recognize the results of the labors of these helpers. Of course, it takes a good set of sensible eyes and ears to notice them.

生徒会長

12

Seito Kaicho
(Student Representative)

"YES, MA'AM. YES … but, but … ahem." The student representative tries to answer the questions of an inquirer in the lobby who looks more interested in the student representative than in the answers he is giving! Being a martial arts *dojo* attracts all kinds of people, and once in a while we receive a visitor whose views on the martial arts are not quite the same as our own.

Nippon Kan has two student representatives: one holds the chair position, and the other acts as an alternate when needed. The duty of the student representative is to facilitate communication between students and staff. His or her job is to listen to problems a student may be having, to answer questions, or to address complaints. They must be able to pass directives and decisions from the office staff to the student body on policy issues when needed, and keep the staff informed of any student concerns. The representatives are selected from younger black belt students active in *dojo* activities who are familiar with both the office staff and students. Being chair representative sounds like an impressive title, but in reality it can be a very tough job. Relaying information diplomatically and problem-solving are not always easy tasks.

The *dojo* is open to all potential new students and everyone is welcome. With so many students, however, occasionally there is an individual who does not fit comfortably within the group. The *dojo* does have policies on conduct and appearance for the safety and comfort of all students. New students may not be aware that their work-out clothes need to be washed a little more frequently for the comfort of their partners, or that their make-up and perfume ends up all over everyone else when they practice. Some try to wear jewelry onto the mat and are reluctant to remove it when cautioned. Students who seem unable to conform to these guidelines are monitored until it can be determined if they will be able to adapt to policy standards. To help with these delicate situations, the student representative acts as an important liaison. It is up to the student representative to make sure that students are made aware of *dojo* rules as diplomatically as possible. The job also entails lending an experienced ear to younger students upset by the outcome of a ranking promotion, or talking to students who have not been keeping up with their dues.

The position of student representative offers valuable training towards becoming a good manager in any situation. Once again, Aikido training extends beyond the mat.

hair pulled straight
back into a ponytail
(new instructors)

frayed
shoulders

frayed
collar

Bleached white
from many washes.

tied like an old
West gun belt
below the
navel.

Instructor
patch

Hair worn off
muscular wrists

Palms full of weapon
calluses

Black belt
faded, ready to fall
apart
(Now pre stonewash
black belts are
available)

Uniform pants cut
off above the knee

Hakama worn white
in front from knee walking

指導員

13 *Shidoin*
(Instructors)

WITHOUT WARNING, A black belt student is told he is
to become part of the instructing staff which is made up of instructors
and assistant instructors. There is no prior notice from the office that
this decision has been made. As the student enters the *dojo* to participate in regular practice, they are advised, "As of today, you will be part
of the instructing staff as an assistant instructor." Of course, this decision was not made randomly. As chief instructor, I also rely on the office
staff to keep a very close watch on instructor candidates for a period
of time before making such a decision.

"Instructing is learning" is another Nippon Kan motto. Sometimes
if the candidate is not quite ready for such a responsibility, it can have
an adverse effect on his or her attitude and performance. Being a good

learner and delivering techniques smoothly is one thing, but having the ability to be a good instructor—to be able to lead a class of many students through a safe and productive work-out—is quite another. Instructor candidates are observed in their participation in out-of-*dojo* activities as well as in-class practice. Personality is a strong consideration as well as technical ability.

It is very important for instructors to be able to maintain a certain distance from students while working closely with them. This is especially true when relating to beginning students in activities on and off the mat. Instructors are advised not to mix their responsibilities as part of the instructing staff with their private affairs. Punctuality is also important. Class must begin and end exactly on time. This requires a sense of professionalism. Running over the allotted time for class does not so much indicate an instructor's enthusiasm for teaching his or her class as it shows a lack of planning and organization. The patch that instructors and assistant instructors wear on the sleeve of their uniform signifies additional responsibilities at Nippon Kan and they are expected to behave as leaders in the *dojo*.

Occasionally, the instructing staff gather after class over a cold beer to discuss their classes, ways to improve their teaching technique, and any problems they might be facing. Being an instructor at Nippon Kan sounds good, but the responsibility must be taken seriously. As part of the *dojo* management structure, if an instructor has problems controlling his or her class with proper authority, office staff must be answered to. Responsibilities get heavier at this stage of training.

14 *Sanyaku*
(Directors)

THE FACES OF these three people, the directors of Nippon Kan, are not shown here. If I were not to draw their faces to their liking, who knows what the consequences would be? In other words, these people are my bosses—and I have even had nightmares of being sent back to Japan!

Not only these directors, but all students who have been students at Nippon Kan for over fifteen years hold a special position of honor and respect in the *dojo*. Some senior students, because of their outside responsibilities, cannot attend practice regularly. But their presence is still extremely valuable, and their position in the *dojo* is very high. They are the veterans who were instrumental in founding the *dojo* and are a treasured part of Nippon Kan's history.

There can only be veteran students if there are beginning students to support them. Likewise, there can be no beginning students without the support of senior members. A balanced relationship between the two is what makes a *dojo* strong and healthy. If a *dojo* is mostly made up of senior students, a common problem occurs—it is difficult to keep beginning students involved. It is very important to keep a balance between the number of beginning and advanced students; there cannot be one without the other. Senior students can attract more beginning students by understanding and respecting what beginning students bring to the *dojo*. Being a good leader begins with a sense of responsibility and pride in the *dojo*, something beginners need for their own growth as students and productive members. Relying on this strength, the balance created runs full circle and results in a healthy *dojo*.

顧問会

15 *Komon Kai*
(Advisors)

THE *Komon Kai* is composed of individuals who may not have a direct link with the daily operations of the *dojo,* but, due to their accomplishments and respected position in the community, they serve as advisors and offer invaluable advice and guidance. To be asked to be a member of the advisory committee has nothing to do with Aikido rank. As a matter of fact, there are committee members who have never even practiced Aikido. This is actually an important aspect of the advisory committee. It is easy to fall into a pattern of consulting only with people within the Aikido community, and this can be a limitation. In order to break away from this tendency and keep informed of new directions and ideas, it is essential to have members on the advisory committee whose expertise lies in other areas.

It is vital to be kept informed on what is happening on many levels, in many areas, to keep up with the times. It is important to be aware of local and worldwide issues and to discuss both the causes of and proposed solutions to those issues. When trying to understand current events of such diversity, people outside of the Aikido community can offer great insight. Precious information gathered during a committee meeting is often reflected in the following day's instruction.

Guest speakers from different fields of expertise are often invited to a *Komon Kai* meeting. Old and new topics are discussed over a specially-prepared meal. This special dinner usually takes two days of planning and preparing. As chief instructor, I do this personally because I want to offer the best hospitality possible for these special guests. These meetings offer me the opportunity to listen to the quality advice and intelligent views of others. In this way, I can formulate a more educated strategy toward continuing and developing the practice of Aikido in the United States. These issues are vital to me personally.

Behind the development and prosperity of Nippon Kan there has been so much support—materially, financially, and in terms of vast human resources. Some day, I hope to be able to return all the favors and kindness to those who have graciously given so much.

16 Kancho
(Chief of Nippon Kan)

THIS IS MY title. I am the *cho* (chief) of Nippon Kan. The word *kan* means "large house," therefore I am *Kancho*. There can only be a *cho* if there are many who surround him. There can only be a *Kancho* if there are many students. No one can be a *Kancho* by themselves.

Being the *Kancho* of Nippon Kan is sometimes like being the "Maytag Repairman." Because the Nippon Kan staff does such an excellent job managing the *dojo,* I sometimes feel the way he is depicted in advertisements as having nothing to do because his company's products are made so well. Frankly, I have that same kind of faith in the student staff of Nippon Kan.

There are occasions when a Maytag repairman does get called on, and likewise I, too, have a job to do. Actually, I have plenty to do without worrying about how the *dojo* is being managed. It does seem, though, that my role in managing the *dojo* is getting smaller every day and I am proud of that fact. I can now sleep peacefully due to all of the students who have joined forces in taking care of the *dojo*, and I am very grateful. The prosperity of Nippon Kan is due to the support and teamwork of many, many people. When people join together, there is power. Teamwork provides both the foundation and the power to develop and realize plans and ideas. My position as *Kancho* exists because of the team and I realize the benefit of this teamwork.

Spelled phonetically in Japanese, *kancho* can also mean the captain of a ship; *kan* in this case means "ship." No matter how magnificent the ship, a captain cannot sail it without a crew. In the same sense, the word *kancho* can also apply to a *dojo*.

There is another meaning for this word in Japanese. Spelled the same but pronounced differently, *kancho* is also the word for "enema." If you are not sure which pronunciation is correct for the situation, it may be better not to use this word.

August 14, 1992
Gaku....Yutaka, I need you to do the sketch for the Japan Branch section.
Yutaka...But I can't draw!
Gaku....Sure you can, just do your best.

November 9, 1992
Gaku....Hello? Did you finish the sketch?
Yutaka..Well, not quite. Why don't you do it, any thing will be just fine..
Gaku....Are you sure? Anything is fine?
Yutaka..Yes, if you please.

June 18, 1993
Gaku....Did you get my fax of the sketch I drew for you?
Yutaka...Yes, I did receive it...but I'm not sure what it is?
Gaku....It's you, the Japan Branch coordinator! You said anything was okay!

日本支部

17 *Nippon Shibu* (Japan Branch)

OFTEN, VOLUNTEERS FROM Japan come to visit us in Denver for short periods of time. As part of their crosscultural exchange experience, they volunteer in the Nippon Kan office and participate in *dojo* activities and projects. One of the goals of Nippon Kan's Federal nonprofit crosscultural exchange program is to give young Japanese people a firsthand opportunity to experience life in America. Their stays vary in length from one month to one year, and Nippon Kan acts as their sponsor.

Since Nippon Kan has often been highlighted in Japanese news media, young people there write frequently to ask if they can join in our activities. Some visitors drop by while touring the United States. Over the years, we have had over 200 visitors from Japan. Interestingly,

I would not claim that all of our visitors returned to Japan satisfied with their experience at Nippon Kan. As I have explained, life at our *dojo* is in some ways even more traditional than contemporary Japanese life. Compounded by being expected to actively participate in all our projects and activities, this is sometimes too much for some young people to handle.

More often than not, our visitors from Japan do accomplish their goals at Nippon Kan and make a valuable contribution here. When it is time for them to return to Japan, their presence is deeply missed. Yutaka Kikuchi, who cofounded Nippon Kan, returned to Japan in 1986. Under his leadership, the Japan branch of Nippon Kan was established in the spring of 1991. Today members of the Japan branch live all over Japan and offer a network of assistance with Nippon Kan's activities. Our overseas members keep us updated on Japanese current events, coordinate travel arrangements when Nippon Kan members visit Japan, and assist with Nippon Kan's many publishing projects.

V

陰徳業編

Other Aspects of the Dojo

1 *Jyo Setsu*
(Snow Removal)

EACH OF DENVER'S four seasons is quite beautiful, although the summers are very hot and winters can be extremely cold. This range of conditions, however, is ideal for Aikido training. During the winter months, it is unusual to have snow for days on end without a bit of sunshine, but occasionally there is a heavy storm that leaves behind a thick blanket of snow. The *uchideshi* and the students who arrive early for class share the job of clearing the walks and parking areas of snow before classes begin. Since weekend classes begin at 8:30 in the morning, a few hearty souls arrive around 7:00 A.M. on snowy days to begin shoveling. Arriving with shovels in hand, it is clear that these volunteers planned the night before to begin this outside "practice."

When a severe snowstorm hits, icy roads make driving through traffic a dangerous proposition. During such a storm, the telephone at the *dojo* rings continuously. "Are you holding classes this evening?" a student calls to ask. "The *dojo* is always here, but more important is the question of your safety. If you have to drive, it might be better for you to stay home," replies the office staff person.

Without fail, there are a few dedicated students who walk to the *dojo* bundled up in heavy clothing. "For you Aikido-holic students, dinner will be served tonight after practice!" I announce. After practice has ended, the *uchideshi* and the students who braved the elements to get to the *dojo* sit together engaged in discussions about Aikido—and life in general—over warming drinks.

How one perceives, accepts, and acts upon what is going on around them is key to understanding daily life. This phenomenon can be seen in tasks as small as shoveling snow. To watch two students negotiate who gets to use the snow shovel first is a sight that warms the heart.

農園作務

2 Noen Samu
(The Garden at Work)

A MEETING WAS taking place in a corner of the garden. "There I was," lamented the earthworm, "minding my own business when all of a sudden—with a shout—the commotion began. The way they started plowing, they must be amateurs—it is going to be a long summer, I just know it!" A cucumber seed joins in, "They planted me so deep, it was quite a struggle just to reach the surface. Once I got here, I was shocked to find that many of my fellow sprouts were being pulled as weeds!" Droplets of water chimed in, "First they forgot how important it was that we get to the garden, and then when they remembered, they had us running all night long. They definitely haven't gotten their watering routine figured out!" From across the way, a horse sauntered by to comment, "What on earth are they using for fertilizer in your garden—that isn't horse manure, is it? Oh, how embarrassing. They sure don't understand what horsepower is *supposed* to mean!"

The sun was up in the sky watching over this meeting, and began to intervene. "I am sure they are trying their best with the little knowledge and experience they have. I was watching them, and at least their intentions seem good. Why don't we all join forces and give our greenhorn gardeners a good harvest? That should please everyone."

An additional plot for the vegetable garden project, leased from the City and County of Denver, is located about ten minutes from the *dojo*. The staff of volunteer gardeners take turns looking after this site. During summer months, the sun shines down on the garden unmercifully and if someone forgets to water at the right time, the plants dry up and sometimes even burn. The volunteers take turns watering the garden before they go to work (dressed in suits and dresses), or after work before they come to the *dojo* for practice.

Since experience is not a requirement, there are more than a few beginning gardeners. In fact, beginners are encouraged to participate. Many amusing stories have grown from the garden along with the vegetables. There is the story of the new volunteer who unwittingly overwatered after seeding, causing all the seeds to float away. More than once, young sprouts have been pulled as weeds. The volunteers learn a lot about the garden under the patient guidance of the staff leader. Working hard carrying fertilizer and preparing the beds for planting, he always has time to pass on a secret tip of gardening: "Tend to the plants with gentle care from your heart."

In the process of growing vegetables, nature has much to teach us about the meaning of life. Rock-hard eggplants and wormeaten cabbages don't really matter. The produce actually harvested is a secondary benefit to the experience gained from gardening.

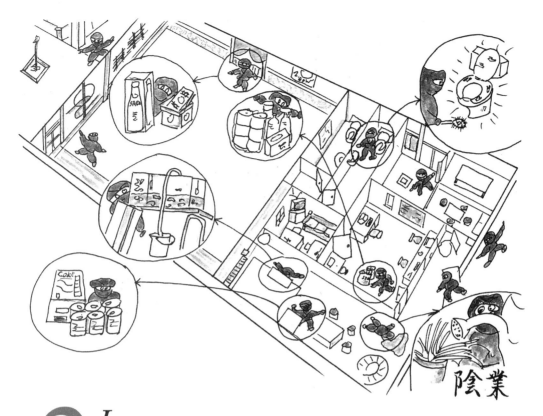

陰業

3 *Ingyo*
(Anonymous Acts of Kindness)

"THERE MUST BE a *ninja* in the *dojo*." "No, there can't be." "Yes, I think there is, it has to be a *ninja*."

Beautifully arranged flowers appear regularly, plants are kept watered, the fish tank is maintained, and the toilets are always scrubbed clean. Sodas in the vending machine are replenished and frequently a donation is left quietly in the *shomen* (altar in the front of the *dojo*). Closets remain full of cleaning supplies and toiletry items.

Who is managing all of these tasks? Where do all of the supplies come from, and when are they stocked? Since all of these tasks are performed without anyone noticing, some think it is the work of a *dojo ninja*.

There really aren't any *ninja* in the *dojo*. All of these tasks are performed by the many individuals who volunteer their time and effort toward keeping the *dojo* beautiful and well-maintained. They do this on their own without being asked, with never a thought of recognition for their contributions. Students who away from the *dojo* are supervisors in large corporations quietly scrub the sinks and toilets. One senior student spends half an hour every week cleaning the fish tank. A small souvenir from an out-of-state business trip is placed on the *shomen*. An envelop containing a donation with a card saying simply "Thank You" is also placed there anonymously. A large bag left in the lobby is filled with rolls of toilet paper and cleaning supplies—no one knows who brought them.

Whenever I have the opportunity, I thank these individuals for their generous actions in front of all students. "A number of people have been very generous in many ways in their support of this *dojo*. I respect your wishes to remain anonymous, but I am clearly aware of your actions. My eyes have not been blind to your good deeds. Even if you wish to keep your *ninja* mask on, I do know who you are and do not forget what you have done."

The actions of these *ninja* are an enormous help toward the successful operation of this *dojo*, and to them I say, "*Domo arigato gozaimasu*" ("Thank you very much").

4 Shuzen (Repair Work)

STUDENTS LIE OR sit in strange postures on the mat, concentrating on the task at hand. After a few minutes of observation, it finally comes to me. "This looks like the rock garden at the Ryoanji Temple in Kyoto!" Watching them repair the badly worn mat reminds me of the beauty of a rock garden.

The mat at Nippon Kan *dojo* is made up of a layer of foam rubber covered with a canvas drawn tightly to each of the four sides with rope. Every four or five years, the canvas needs to be replaced. The *dojo* currently has its fourth canvas. Of course, no one is allowed onto the mat with shoes or allowed to carry sharp objects that might cause a tear, but just like the knees in a favorite pair of jeans, after five years of use even heavy canvas shows signs of wear. Late in the evening after practice students get together to repair the mat. Off come sweaty uniform jackets and students sprawl here and there as the sewing begins. The canvas is pulled taut; it is not easy to pull both sides of a rip together so it can be mended.

Each old *dojo* canvas was repaired many times with patches sewn over some of the larger holes. This was not an issue of not having enough money to buy a new mat. The old canvas taught students a great deal about appreciating and taking care of things and about keeping the *dojo* in good working order, and this had an interesting effect on students. Coincidentally, students began patching their uniforms for a much longer period before buying a new one. Also, handmade carrying cases for *bokken* and *jo* began to appear.

A framed piece of an old section of canvas that was mended many times is kept in the *dojo* as a reminder of the spirit to appreciate what we have. Smaller pieces of the old mat were framed for students to keep as their own souvenirs. Donations made for these momentos paid for our last canvas, which already has its own share of patches.

Throwing away an old pair of sneakers as soon as a new pair has been bought is not a usual habit of an Aikido student. I would expect an Aikido student to feel a bit sad about seeing the old pair go, and hope they would offer a "thank you" for their many months of wear.

5 *Kifu*
(Donations)

ONE MORNING I heard a rather loud noise outside the *dojo,* so I went to see what was going on. To my surprise, a huge crate had been left outside the front door. The gentleman who had donated this large object said over his shoulder as he turned to leave, "I'll be back after work to hook it up." Inside the crate was a brand new, bright red jacuzzi bathtub. For the next few days, he returned to work diligently on installing the tub, creating a wonderful bathing room. As president of his own plumbing company, he probably doesn't have to do physical work on a job if he does not want to. Yet he did this installation himself without expecting any words of appreciation from fellow students. It is quite apparent that this student's generous and hardworking personality is the driving force behind his very successful and growing company.

In general, everything Nippon Kan has become is the result of donations. Office staff and instructors are volunteers who donate their time. Furniture and equipment from desks to computers have also been donated. The *dojo* is sustained by donations of time, talent, and material supplies from many sources. As a way of recognizing this support, Nippon Kan students work on various public service projects to give back to the community what has been so generously given. These volunteer projects help both students and members of the greater community to understand Nippon Kan's philosophy, which in turn serves to strengthen the *dojo*. *Wago* (harmony) is an Aikido philosophy spoken of frequently by the founder Morihei Ueshiba, and it is practiced actively at Nippon Kan.

陰德

6 *Intoku*
(The Secret of Virtuous Actions)

THERE ARE MANY aspects of Nippon Kan that I have not been able to address in these pages, and the people I was not able to mention must not be forgotten. As this *dojo* continues to grow there will be even more pages to add someday.

There are some who might think that my lifestyle is one of wealth and luxury. However, as many know, I still don't own a car nor do I have any credit cards. The only plastic card I carry is a membership card to a video shop. I am the chief instructor of Nippon Kan, but I am not its president or vice president. As the only person paid by Nippon Kan, I earn enough to cover simple needs: food, clothing, and a place to live. This having been clarified, I must admit that I actually lead a very fortunate life; indeed, a rich and luxurious life compared to many. The days and months I have spent writing this book have been full and gratifying.

There is a proverb that teaches, "Those who act in good will, they will be rewarded by heaven with fortune." In interpreting this proverb, fortune can either be perceived as being material or as some sort of spiritual enrichment. Regardless of its form, how much fortune one receives depends entirely on the individual.

Each activity of Nippon Kan has added to the richness of my life and I have come to realize that the truest fortune is not material. Fortune lies right where we are standing, if we just take the time to look for it. Even if we recognize our good fortune, what is more important is whether we make the effort to reach out and utilize it. This effort, I'd say, is much easier than trying to catch rainbows high in the sky.

7 *Takaramono*
(Treasure)

THIS IS MY treasure chest. Inside are the gifts of talent and heart from all those around me. This treasure is greater than any amount of money or position I could attain. With these treasures, many dreams have been realized. This time, too, my dream has come true. Thank you, everyone, from the bottom of my heart.

Afterword

WITH THE TREMENDOUS efforts and support of many people—my translator Yutaka Kikuchi, editor and project coordinator Emily Busch, technical editor Diane DeVries, and the staff of Nippon Kan and Frog Ltd./North Atlantic Books—I have been able to produce this book. With the support and inspiration of students and staff I have been able to take the time to work in the garden, write books, and work on new projects.

Jetting around the country teaching seminars seems like a nice life for a chief instructor, but now it is my time to stay home and take care of those who have offered me so much opportunity. I have much to learn by staying home. My title is Chief Instructor, but essentially I am simply another student on the path of practice. Everyday thinking, everyday doing, everyday learning and changing—this is the obligation of my practice.

Nippon Kan continues to grow. But it is not my style to sit back and do nothing. By the time this book has been published I will no doubt be working on yet another challenging project.

Fundamental to martial artists is the concept of the "way"—not staying in one place. This is the "*do*" in "*Aikido,*" and it is also my path or "way."

Let's see, now what's next?!